THE PROMISE

Gerhard F. Hasel
Michael G. Hasel

Pacific Press®
Publishing Association
Nampa, Idaho | www.pacificpress.com

Dedication

To Hilde,
a most supportive wife and mother
who has demonstrated a Christian life to her family.

Contents

One

God, Creation, and Covenant

"In the beginning God created the heavens and the earth" (Genesis 1:1, RSV). With these majestic words, human beings are introduced to God as Creator, whom we later come to know also as Redeemer.[1]

This sentence includes four basic ideas. First, it introduces God. The great thinker Immanuel Kant once wrote that in all philosophy, there are but three great problems—the greatest of which is the problem of the existence of God. The first verse of Scripture reveals God's existence.

Second, the verb of the sentence *created* (*bā rā'*) always indicates God's activity: God created. This means that the God who created reveals Himself in creative activities. The word *created* indicates how God as Creator made the world; He made the world through His creative activity.

Third, the expression "the heavens and the earth" is used in the same sequence or in reversed order forty-one times in the Old Testament, indicating that this phrase refers to our earth and its surrounding heavenly atmospheres. Here the question is answered as to what was created.

Finally, we come to the opening words, "In the beginning." These words tell us when God created "the heavens and the earth."

This first sentence goes far beyond philosophy's greatest problem, for it answers four basic questions: who? how? what? and when? Genesis 1:1

addresses the very core questions of human existence by providing information about God, our planet and its surrounding atmospheres, the way in which our globe came into existence, and the time when it came into existence.[2]

The Bible does not prove that God is Creator—it reveals that He is Creator. Without this revelation, we would never have known that this world was created by God. Without this revelation, we would never have known the purpose of our life on earth.

The Bible clearly reveals that God the Father was the Originator of the creation (1 Corinthians 8:6; Ephesians 3:9; Hebrews 1:2), and it also reveals that Jesus Christ, the Second Person of the triune Godhead, is the Agent of creation (John 1:3; Ephesians 3:9; Hebrews 1:2). The Bible plainly affirms that God did not create out of a need to fulfill Himself (Isaiah 40:12–31), for He was exactly the same after Creation as He was in Himself before (Psalm 90:2). God the Creator is self-contained and self-sufficient and not part of His creation; He stands as the transcendent God above and beyond His creation.

God's creation is described in Genesis 1 and 2 as "good." He "saw everything that he had made, and, behold, it was very good" (Genesis 1:31, ASV). God's creatorship and God's goodness belong together from the beginning.

Throughout the Bible the Creator is presented as the triune God. The Creator is the everlasting God and Lord. By Jesus Christ all things in heaven and earth (Ephesians 3:9) were created (Colossians 1:16). By the Word (Jesus) the world was made; "without him was not any thing made that was made" (John 1:3). The "Spirit of God moved upon the face of the waters" (Genesis 1:2).

The place of man in Creation

In the biblical story of Creation, "man" (*'ādām*, a generic noun referring to human beings or people) is represented as the crowning climax of Creation. More emphasis is placed on the creation of man than on any other aspect of Creation in chapter 1. The second chapter of Genesis is an intricate expansion on this climax theme.[3]

Indeed, the creation of man is the result of divine deliberation within the triune Godhead. This is expressed for the first time in the plural of *deliberation* used in Genesis 1:26: "Let us make man." No other creative act is preceded by such "God with God" deliberation. Man's lofty place in creation is, thus, established from the beginning.[4]

Human beings are the only earthly creature that God created in His own image and after His own likeness. The words "image of God" profoundly express that man's external resemblance, his character, and his mental, spiritual, and moral capacities are reflecting the divine image. All of this suggests the immense dignity and worth, authority and responsibility, with which human beings are endowed in creation.

The statements that man is made in the "image of God," that he has been created "after our likeness," reveals, on the one hand, closeness between God and man and, on the other hand, the basic distance between God and man (Genesis 1:27, 26). Man was not created to be another god or the god over the earth. God is Creator and man is creature— but not creature on the level of an animal, even if one thought of a superior animal. Man is a creature in God's likeness and image. Man, created in the image and likeness of God, is set fully apart, not only from the animals but also from Deity.

Being created in the image and likeness of God was not Adam's privilege only. Both male and female were created in the image and likeness of God. In creation no distinction of rank or importance existed between man and woman—they were equal. Both man and woman find their full meaning, not in a superior-inferior relationship but in their mutual relationship and in their common, vital communion with God.

Man is indeed a new order of being. Because God created man and woman in His image and likeness, a most profound communion and a most meaningful relationship could exist between Him and human beings. This God-man relationship is God's fantastic gift to humanity. God made people so that this relationship would exist and could grow throughout the ages. Human beings are the crown of Creation because they have been made especially to enjoy fellowship and communion with their Creator.

Initiator of communion with man

In the first two chapters of the Bible, which describe the time and events before sin entered the world, we find explicit evidence that God the Creator established communion with man and woman. In Genesis 1:28 we read, "God blessed them." Before God spoke to Adam and Eve, He "blessed them." The divine blessing is a free, undeserved gift of God involving well-being and prosperity, a wholeness rooted in God and experienced in everyday life.

The profound, unhindered, and undisturbed communion of the God-man relationship could never be complete and total if man did not have free choice to live within such a relationship.

While Adam and Eve's highest calling was to serve God, they were unique in being the only creatures who could respond to God in obedience as well as disobedience, in faith and trust as well as in rebellion and distrust. Unlike the animal creation, which obeys on the basis of instinctive impulses and laws, man and woman were given the freedom of will as part of their mental and spiritual heritage. Man and woman were given the possibility of separating themselves from God just as easily as they could maintain fellowship with Him. By their God-given choice, Adam and Eve "could obey and live, or disobey and perish."[5]

This choice was highlighted by that special tree, and only one at that, from which the first pair was not to eat. "But of the tree of the knowledge of good and evil you shall not eat, for in the day that you eat of it you shall die" (Genesis 2:17, RSV).

The test of fellowship

The test provided in the form of the tree of the knowledge of good and evil indicated that man's relationship to God depended on free choice. No test existed if men and women were not free to say yes or no to God.

The test would show that man was not superman and that he would function best only in dependence upon his Maker. The test would demonstrate whether man would wish to be like God and thus abandon his dependent role and status inherent in being created in the image of God. The test would reveal that man's relationship with God can be effective and lasting only if man freely chooses to live and function in that beneficent relationship. To reject the relationship would mean that man would attempt to live independently from God, thinking that he had no need of God. But to break the relationship was also to know evil, to experience alienation and loneliness and all the pain of separation in a life apart from God.

The Creation narrative of Genesis 1:1 to 2:4 and the complementary story of the creation of Adam and Eve in their perfect environment provided in Genesis 2:4–25 contain no hint of foreboding that would in any way suggest a threat to God's perfect creation. Everything in these two narratives has the seal of perfection stamped on it. Until man and woman disobeyed God, the future was one of continuous and unhindered fellowship with Him.

Our first parents failed the test of love, faith, and obedience. "When the woman saw that the tree was good for food, and that it was a delight to the eyes, and that the tree was to be desired to make one wise, she took of its fruit and ate; and she also gave some to her husband, and he ate. Then the eyes of both were opened" (Genesis 3:6, 7, RSV). The tree that God had placed in the Garden was not inherently evil. It contained no deadly virus or bacteria in some special fruit. The evil was in listening to the wrong person. Eve listened to the serpent, whom Satan was using as his medium (2 Corinthians 11:3, 14), and Adam listened to his wife. Neither listened to God! Thus sin disrupted the life-giving, God-man relationship. Sin stopped open communion.

God, in His creative speaking and doing, brought about a loving, gracious relationship. But man, in deafness and disobedience, destroyed it. Man's disregard of the divine command, "You shall not eat" (Genesis 2:17), indicates that sin is an act of transgressing God's will. This rebel

11

act manifests man's desire to be his own "lord," that he himself wants to decide what is good and evil. Adam and Eve's sin revealed their distrust of God's design for their well-being.

Sin's change of relationships

Man's sin blemished all phases of life on earth (Romans 8:21, 22). Genesis 3 explains in verses 7, 10, and 11–13 that several major changes took place on account of man's sin. First, the relationship between man and woman was broken, marked by an emergency action of sewing together fig leaves. Second, the relationship between man and the created world was interrupted and became marked by fear, alienation, and death (Romans 8:19–23; 2 Peter 3:13). Third, the relationship between God and man was decisively interrupted. Man was made for fellowship and communion with God. After sin, Adam and Eve fled from God's face and hid themselves (Genesis 3:8–10); thus wholesome communion was turned into bitter alienation and painful separation.

The biblical teaching on the fall of man opposes many popular conceptions. The modern conception of man as a product of slow, evolutionary, upward development is not supported by the biblical teaching of man's fall into sin. The biblical picture of the Fall thus contradicts the evolutionary scheme of man slowly rising from primeval fear and groping ignorance to proud heights of religious sensitivity and insight. The Bible does not portray man as risen but as fallen—a created being in desperate and continual need of a saving God.

Reestablishment of the God-man relationship

The immense tragedy of man's decision to yield to the evil one—a decision that led to an almost obliterated "image of God"—did not cause the Creator to turn from Adam and Eve in their desperate need. Would a father or mother who first gazes into the face of their child and sees reflected in its eyes an image of themselves, neglect that baby during the time of its greatest need and helplessness? Even then, the same Christ who stooped down to breathe life into Adam's lungs, stepped into action to save the creature who now had turned and was hiding from Him.

God again took the initiative. The marvelous story of God's love unfolded in His Word is that He is always the Initiator, actively seeking man's attention and redemption. As Adam and Eve were hiding before God in fear, guilt, and shame, with marks of sin already within and around them, God approached them with the searching love call, "Where are you?" (Genesis 3:9, RSV). No one in this world can possibly escape from this question.

The searching question "Where are you?" is not a curse, condemnation, or judgment. Rather, we hear God calling the sinner back to a redeeming relationship. Here the Creator is also the Redeemer. Although Creation preceded Redemption, both have belonged together in God's heart from the beginning.

Only the serpent and the ground are cursed (verses 14, 17, 19). The question "Where are you?" was designed to draw guilt-stricken man back into the arms of God. As Derek Kidner observed, "God's first words to fallen man have all the marks of grace. It is a question, since to help him [man] He must draw rather than drive him out of hiding."[6]

The initial reaching out on the part of God toward Adam and Eve did not end in Eden. Down to our day, to this moment, the Lord continues to reach out to His creatures. The story of redemption is a recurring double theme: Sin breaks the beneficent God-man relationship (the closest possible fellowship that can be conceived by the human mind). Immediately the divine Initiator of that relationship begins the process of breaking through the barrier caused by sin and Satan to reestablish the lost fellowship with fallen man. At the moment of grief and guilt, shame and frustration, alienation and separation, God's love reaches across the gulf of separation caused by sin—Adam's and our own—to bring us back into His loving arms. The apostle Peter perceptively reveals, "The Lord is not slack concerning his promise, as some men count slackness; but is long-suffering to us-ward, not willing that any should perish, but that all should come to repentance" (2 Peter 3:9).

Provision for salvation

In Genesis 3:15 God's surprising word of prophetic hope speaks of a divinely ordained hostility—"I will put enmity" between the serpent (Satan) and the woman, between his seed and her seed (RSV). This enmity climaxes the victorious appearance of a "He," a representative offspring of the woman's seed, who delivers a lethal blow to the head of Satan. Thus the first promise in the Bible speaks of One who will effectively break the power of the tempter.

This Messianic promise gave Adam and Eve hope in their desperation. This hope transformed their existence because it was a God-given, God-guaranteed hope. This hope of the Messiah and of final victory transcends all other hope. It is built on the promise of a renewed relationship with God, one of grace and mercy, forgiveness and salvation, pardon and power.

Thus, the beginning of Scripture tells us not only the story of Creation but also the story of redemption—the story of a covenantal relationship between God and man. God can be Redeemer only because He is Creator.

Human philosophy caused a separation between the doctrine of Creation and the special revelation of God, making the study of creation a matter of natural theology. The Bible clearly depicts Creation as the beginning of history; both Creation and history are inseparably related and linked to each other.[7] Creation is the foundation of the covenant and covenantal relationship between God and man. Thus it is not correct to say that the covenant is the rational principle or the ground of Creation. The biblical picture of Creation is prior to the covenant, and the covenant finds its meaning and its completion in relationship to Creation, not vice versa.

---

1. On the uniqueness of the biblical Creation account, see Gerhard F. Hasel and Michael G. Hasel, "The Unique Cosmology of Genesis 1 against Ancient Near Eastern and Egyptian Parallels," in *The Genesis Creation Account and Its Reverberations in the Old Testament*, ed. Gerald A. Klingbeil (Berrien Springs, MI: Andrews University Press, 2015), 9–29; and on the theology, see further articles in the same volume.

2. On the technical aspects of this verse, see Gerhard F. Hasel, "Recent Translations of Genesis 1:1: A Critical Look," *The Bible Translator* 22 (1971): 154–167.

3. Frank M. Hasel and Michael G. Hasel, *How to Interpret Scripture* (Nampa, ID: Pacific Press, 2019), 84, 85.

4. Gerhard F. Hasel, "The Meaning of 'Let Us' in Gn 1:26," *Andrews University Seminary Studies* 13 (1975): 58–66.

5. Ellen G. White, *Patriarchs and Prophets* (Mountain View, CA: Pacific Press®, 1958), 53.

6. Derek Kidner, *Genesis: An Introduction and Commentary*, Tyndale Old Testament Commentaries (Chicago: InterVarsity Press, 1967), 70.

7. On theological implications, see Michael G. Hasel, "In the Beginning. . . ." *Adventist Review*, October 25, 2001, 24–27; idem., "Biblical Implications for Accepting a Nonliteral View of Creation," in *The Genesis Creation Account and Its Reverberations in the New Testament*, ed. Thomas Shepherd (Berrien Springs, MI: Andrews University Press, 2020).

Two

God—the Constant Initiator

In 1905 a team of German archaeologists began working to uncover the ancient ruins located near the town of Boğazköy in modern Turkey. The site included an ancient library containing hundreds of texts written in cuneiform. One of the tablets begins by mentioning the "Great King, King of Hatti," which indicates that this is the ancient capital of the Hittite empire![1] In 1931, a language expert published the treaties made between the Hittite princes, confirming that this is the first treaty text found outside the Bible, but it was more than twenty years later that Professor George Mendenhall of the University of Michigan compared it with the covenants found in the contemporary writings of Moses.[2] Professor Mendenhall found that Hittite and biblical treaties contain a number of similarities:

- Preamble introducing the sovereign
- The historical prologue describing previous relations between the contracting parties
- The stipulations that outline the nature of the community formed by the covenant or treaty
- The document clause providing the preservation and regular rereading of the treaty

- The list of gods who witnessed the treaty
- The curse and blessings or blessing formula—curses depending upon infidelity and blessing upon fidelity to the treaty

Many Old Testament scholars have concluded that an apparent formal similarity exists between the Old Testament covenants and the ancient Oriental treaty pattern as manifested particularly by the Hittites.[3] Others feel that this has been shown to be a rather narrow base and that one should exercise a significant measure of caution in comparing treaties between Hittite princes and other rulers with the Old Testament covenants.[4] It is certain that the Old Testament covenant is unique when compared to any ancient secular treaty in several aspects. First, it is only in Scripture that such a contractual agreement or relationship is formalized between God and man. All Near Eastern treaties are between equals or vassals—civil powers or rulers. Second, God, never man, is always the Initiator of the covenant.

Thus the idea of the covenant, one of the most profound biblical concepts, uniquely expresses the deep communion, intimate relationship, and closest fellowship between God and man. In fact, many biblical scholars have considered that the central idea of the Bible, both in the Old Testament and the New, is the covenant.[5] Some have suggested that the covenant theme is the all-encompassing concept that unifies the two testaments of the Bible. However one expresses it, the covenant idea functions as one of the central themes in Scripture.

Covenant terminology

The standard expression in the Old Testament for establishing or making a covenant between God and man is the idiomatic phrase "to make a covenant" (Genesis 15:18; Exodus 24:8; Deuteronomy 4:23; 5:2; Jeremiah 11:10; Ezekiel 34:25; etc.). The Hebrew phrase reads literally "to cut a covenant" *(kārat bᵉrît).* This expression appears in the Old Testament no fewer than 80 times, and the term *covenant (bᵉrît)* itself appears no fewer than 287 times.

The Promise: God's Everlasting Covenant

In the Bible the word *b^erît* is used in two types of relationships. On the one hand, it is used as a designation of a relationship either between human parties of equal standing or between unequal partners. Depending on the status of the contracting parties, *b^erît* can mean in this connection "contract," "bond," "alliance," or "treaty" (Genesis 14:13; 21:22–32; 26:26–31; 1 Samuel 18:3; 20:18; 2 Samuel 3:12, 13; 5:1; 1 Kings 20:34; Hosea 12:1; Ezekiel 17:15; Malachi 2:14; etc.). This kind of covenant has little religious importance in the Old Testament.

The more frequent and most significant usage of the Hebrew term *b^erît*, "covenant," occurs in connection with the covenantal relationship between God and man as in the Noachic, Abrahamic, Mosaic (Sinaitic), Davidic, and "new" covenants. In these instances the covenant is neither a mutually negotiated or agreed-upon contract (bond, treaty, or alliance), nor a divinely imposed obligation. The Hebrew expression *kārat b^erît* (literally, "to cut a covenant") corresponds to a Sumerian expression that means "to cut a ban" (*nam-erim-TAR*). The meaning "to cut" in the Hebrew expression has the idiomatic sense of "make." The original idea built into "to cut a covenant" is the actual practice of killing and then "cutting" (*kārat*) an animal or several animals to establish or ratify the covenant.

Although a comprehensive definition of *covenant* is difficult to formulate, this definition will be useful in understanding the chapters that follow: In the divine-human situation, covenant is a divinely initiated and sovereign-ordained relationship between God and man in which God as superior Lord graciously discloses, confirms, and fulfills the covenant promise. Man, as beneficiary of the divine covenant gifts, freely accepts the enduring relationship and renders obedience to the divine obligations (commandments, statutes, laws, or ordinances) through the assisting and enabling grace provided by God.

God—the Initiator of the Noachic covenant

The noun *covenant* (*b^erît*) is found in the Bible for the first time in Genesis 6:18. The speaker is God, and Noah is the one addressed. A divine decision had been made—God would virtually bring to an end the work He wrought in Creation, described earlier in Genesis. The reason—a massive and sustained spread of sin that was climaxed in the corrupt world of Noah's day.

God's judgment would come in the form of a worldwide flood. Yet God had still committed Himself to the world He had created. He had not forsaken those who had not forsaken Him. So God, in fulfilling His divine purpose, made a covenant as an expression of His relationship with Noah.

The divine, redemptive purpose of the covenant relationship that had been in operation since the Fall (Genesis 3:15) is here renewed by God taking the initiative: "I will establish my covenant with you" (Genesis 6:18, RSV). The divine "I" of the covenant initiative is Noah's ground of security in the impending crisis. God establishes the covenant. The origin and initiation of the covenant relationship is fully grounded and secured in God. Man is the beneficiary of this relationship, demonstrating once again that salvation is from the Lord.

God's redemptive initiative for man's well-being is clearly expressed in the covenant passages of Genesis 6:19 and Genesis 9:8–10. These divine initiatives are God's reaffirmation of His original saving intentions for the human family.

God—the Initiator of the Abrahamic covenant

God spread His covenant making with Abraham over various periods of time. In Genesis 12:1–3, we find a fivefold "I will" (RSV) on the part of God, revealing the intensity and greatness of God's commitment to Abraham. Abraham received but a single, searching command, "Go forth" (verse 1, NASB). Abraham obeyed by faith, according to Hebrews 11:8, not in order to bring about the blessing promised by God but as a response of faith on his part that corresponded to the gracious relationship that God was about to establish with him. "Abraham's unquestioning obedience is one of the most striking evidences of faith to be found in all the Bible."[6] Although there can be no covenant fellowship and no blessing without obedience, obedience is a faith response on the part of the believer and the result of God's prior enabling action. Obedience is not the means to earn fellowship with God or to gain blessings promised by God—but the result of God's initiative and the fellowship that He has established with us.

God—the Initiator of the Mosaic covenant

God took the initiative in establishing a covenant with the Israelites, whom He was bringing from Egypt to Canaan. For several centuries, the descendants of Abraham, Isaac, and Jacob had lived in Egyptian bondage. "In their bondage the people had to a great extent lost the knowledge of God and of the principles of the Abrahamic covenant."[7] In His kindness, God reestablished the relationship between Himself and the Israelites, which is expressed in the words, "I will take you for my people, and I will be your God" (Exodus 6:7, RSV).

The unfathomable and unexpected initiative on the part of God toward the Israelites in the midst of Egyptian idolatry and corruption, setting them free from degrading slavery and from idolatrous worship, rests in the deep mystery of God's love, mercy, and grace (Deuteronomy 4:37; 7:7–9; 10:15). This mystery of God's saving initiative becomes unfolded in divine revelation and is far beyond the probing of philosophical questions or human investigation.

The source of the covenant relationship lies in God Himself. Redemption from Egyptian slavery and bondage was brought about by God's own mighty power and in His miraculous acts (Exodus 5–12). This graciously performed earthly redemption for the enslaved people precedes God's covenant making and Israel's covenant response, a response in obedience and love. The act of making a covenant with ancient Israel is an act of God's loving-kindness, totally initiated by Him and completely unearned and unmerited by His people.

God—the Initiator of the Davidic covenant

The key passage describing God's covenant with David is recorded in

2 Samuel 7:1–7. In this instance, God's initiative in making a covenant with King David clearly stands in the foreground. God's initiative is neither purchased by David nor conditioned by His desires or ambitions. The psalmist wrote, "Thou hast said, 'I have made a covenant with my chosen one, I have sworn to David my servant: I will establish your descendants for ever, and build your throne for all generations' " (Psalm 89:3, 4, RSV). Notice how the psalmist expresses God's initiative in a fourfold way. Each of these ways introduces the divine "I" followed by an action verb: (1) "I have made a covenant"; (2) "I have sworn"; (3) "I will establish your descendants"; (4) "[I will] build your throne." The first two, "I" statements speak about covenant making, while the following "I" statements contain covenant promises.

The marvelous promise about the Davidic "seed" of 2 Samuel 7:12 calls for further examination. The term *seed* (*zera'*) reflects a familiar theme in the Bible that appeared first in the marvelous promise made by God to Adam and Eve in Genesis 3:15. In this verse *seed* is a singular noun with a flexible reference to the many descendants, the collective offspring, and to the One Person, the single Offspring, who was to come to crush Satan's head. The appearance of the word *seed* in the covenantal promise to Abraham in Genesis 12:7 and its repetition to his son Isaac in Genesis 18:19 and to his son Jacob in Genesis 32:12 and 35:12, is a striking link in the chain that joins the promise made first in Genesis 3:15 to the seed mentioned in connection with King David. In a most narrow sense, the Davidic "seed" came in the form of his son Solomon. However, Solomon was unable to build his kingdom the way it had been predicted, namely, as a kingdom that would stand forever (2 Samuel 7:16). The true "seed" of David was finally and ultimately manifested in the birth of Jesus Christ, who in His life and resurrection established His kingdom forever (Acts 2:30).

God—the Initiator of the new covenant
In Jeremiah 31:31–34 we find the Bible's most profound and exciting promise of the new covenant. This marvelous new-covenant

announcement contains in its first sentence the key theme of God as the divine Initiator of the new covenant, "I will make a new covenant" (Jeremiah 31:31). This reveals that the new covenant, in some way, is in continuity with the previous covenants. The divine fellowship that was God's design for His previous covenants is to be realized in the new covenant, "I . . . will be their God, and they shall be my people" (verse 33).

The perceptive student will note that this is the only passage in the Old Testament in which the covenant God makes a "new covenant." Few people realize that the New Testament received its name from this particular passage. Since the Latin word for covenant is *testament*, Origen, the famous church father (ca. AD 185–254), called the twenty-seven books of the Bible from Matthew to Revelation the New Testament, in order to distinguish between pre-Christian and Christian revelation.

The antiquity of God's initiative in making a covenant with man; in establishing a profound, lasting, and meaningful relationship with man; and in maintaining a vital communion with him, has been stated in this way: "Before the foundations of the earth were laid, the covenant was made that all who were obedient, all who should through the abundant grace provided, become holy in character, and without blame before God, by appropriating that grace, should be children of God."[8]

This covenant of grace initiated in the mind of God long before the foundations of the earth were laid was the covenant that God established with Adam in the Garden of Eden. "The covenant of grace was first made with man in Eden. . . . To all men this covenant offered pardon and the assisting grace of God for future obedience through faith in Christ."[9] This covenant of grace made with the first sinner in the Garden of Eden was the same covenant that God established with Abraham. "This covenant, made from eternity, was given to Abraham hundreds of years before Christ came."[10] The fact that Scripture contains good news for life now and good news for the life to come is the best news for all humanity.

1. Hans G. Güterbock, "Boğazköy," *Oxford Encyclopedia of the Archaeology in the Ancient Near East,* vol. 1 (New York: Oxford University Press, 1997), 333–335.

2. George E. Mendenhall, *Law and Covenant in Israel and the Ancient Near East* (Pittsburgh, PA: Presbyterian Board of Colportage, 1955).

3. K. A. Kitchen and Paul Lawrence, Treaty, *Law and Covenant in the Ancient Near East,* 3 vols. (Wiesbaden: Harrassowitz, 2012); K. A. Kitchen, *On the Reliability of the Old Testament* (Grand Rapids, MI: Eerdmans, 2003).

4. D. J. McCarthy, "Covenant in the OT: The Present State of Inquiry," *Catholic Biblical Quarterly* 27 (1965): 217–240; McCarthy, *Treaty and Covenant,* Analecta biblica 21a (Rome: Biblical Institute Press, 1978).

5. Walther Eichrodt, *Theology of the Old Testament,* vol. 1 (Philadelphia: Fortress, 1961), 13–17; on the wider issues concerning a "center" or unifying theme for the Bible, see Gerhard F. Hasel, "The Problem of the Center in the Old Testament Theology Debate," *Zeitschrift für die alttestamentliche Wissenschaft* 86 (1974): 65–82; Hasel, *Old Testament Theology: Basic Issues in the Current Debate,* 4th ed. (Grand Rapids, MI: Eerdmans, 1991), 139–171.

6. Ellen G. White, *Patriarchs and Prophets* (Mountain View, CA: Pacific Press®, 1958), 126.

7. White, 371.

8. Ellen G. White, *Fundamentals of Christian Education* (Hagerstown, MD: Review and Herald®, 2010), 403.

9. White, *Patriarchs and Prophets,* 370.

10. White, *Fundamentals of Christian Education,* 403.

Three

Flood, Covenant, and Man's Future

A mother drowns her five children in a bathtub and then claims insanity. The world is shut down due to a tiny virus that has infected millions and killed hundreds of thousands. The economy is on the brink of collapse as millions lose their jobs. A blast in Beirut's port creates shockwaves that devastate the city and is felt all the way to neighboring countries. Billions of locusts sweep through Africa and South America consuming all vegetation in their path. These are just a few of the recent headlines that indicate a world spiraling out of control. Yet there was a time when things were even worse.

God described humankind in Noah's day as having so degraded that "every imagination of the thoughts of his heart was only evil continually" (Genesis 6:5). One feels the true impact of this description only within the context of God's declaration at the end of Creation when He pronounced everything "very good" (Genesis 1:31). Sin had so corrupted God's perfect creation that its disintegration had reached fantastic proportions by Noah's time.

Against this background of pre-Flood devastation, let us reflect for a moment upon the nature of sin. Scripture defines sin in a variety of ways, all of which complement each other to give a broad concept of its nature. Sin is rebellion; sin is iniquity; sin is transgression; sin is trespass; sin is lawlessness; sin is unrighteousness. All these definitions include one common characteristic—defiance against God.[1]

The origin, consequences, and spread of sin

The Bible reveals that sin had already invaded the universe before the fall of Adam and Eve. This preexistent satanic power manifested itself through the serpent in the Garden of Eden and seduced the first man and woman into sin. Genesis 3 unfolds the tragic story. "The woman saw that the tree was good for food, and that it was pleasant to the eyes, and a tree to be desired to make one wise" (Genesis 3:6). But sin did not begin with a physical or sensuous lust or even with a lust of the eyes. Such a concept of its entry into this world fails to come to grips with the genius of Satan's assault and the deception by which he ensnared Eve. Satan directed his attack against the integrity and truthfulness of God (verse 4) and seduced Eve by assuring her that she, like God, would know good and evil (verse 5). To be like God means to no longer have need of God. The problem of sin in the Garden of Eden was that Eve gave to Satan the place that belongs only to God; and Adam, in turn, gave that place to Eve. Adam and Eve's transgression meant repudiation of God's authority and doubt about His goodness and wisdom as well as rejection of His justice and contradiction of His truthfulness.

In consequence of sin, man's attitude toward God changed. Now, instead of welcoming His fellowship, Adam and Eve "hid themselves from the presence of the LORD God amongst the trees of the garden" (Genesis 3:8). They also produced for themselves a covering. They now dreaded an encounter with their Lord. Both shame and fear dominated their experience, indicating that a basic disruption in their relationship with God had taken place.

Another consequence of sin showed up in humans' attitude to each other. Adam and Eve, now in a state of fear and shame, began to be alienated from each other (see verse 12).

Sin affected the entire race as death entered the world. God had stated

25

to the first couple that if they ate of the fruit of the tree, they would surely die (Genesis 2:17). Death, in its ultimate sense, means final separation from God. That is what Adam's first sin meant for the whole of the human race (Romans 5:12, 14–19; 1 Corinthians 15:22).

Sin produced consequences that also extended to the physical world. God said, for example, "Cursed is the ground for thy sake" (Genesis 3:17; compare with Romans 8:22). The entire creation felt the repercussions of sin.

From Genesis 4 to Genesis 6:5, a picture of the spread and growth of evil unfolds. Sin destroys like an avalanche. It produces an ever-widening chasm between God and human beings. It moves from disobedience (Genesis 3:1–7) to murder (Genesis 4:8) to reckless killing and titanic lust (verses 23, 24) and on to total corruption and violence (Genesis 6:1–12).

Thus, when God said of Noah's day that "every imagination of the thoughts of his [man's] heart was only evil continually" (Genesis 6:5), He gave a comprehensive assessment. The word *imagination* (from Hebrew *yeser*) means "design," "purpose," or "intent." The word *heart* designates the seat of the thinking and reasoning powers and usually refers to the mind with all its faculties.

What a shocking assessment—men and women's every purpose, intent, and design were only wicked continually!

God's inner reaction

Not frequently in Scripture do we gain an insight into the inner life of God. But Genesis 6:6 gives us such an insight concerning His reaction to the immense, shocking growth of sin. The insight is revealed in two ways. First, God "repented" or "was sorry" (RSV, NASB). This "repentance" is not identical to human repentance. The Hebrew language consistently employs one particular word in the Old Testament in referring to God's repentance—*nācham*. It does not connote a lack of foresight on God's part or any vacillation in His nature or purpose. In this sense, God never repents of anything (1 Samuel 15:29). Neither, of course, does God's repentance involve an aspect of guilt or sin. The word is employed simply to present the truth "that God, in consistency with His immutability, assumes a changed position in respect to changed man."[2]

The second reaction Genesis 6:6 reveals is God's sadness. God was "grieved" in His heart—deeply hurt by humankind and their wickedness. This depiction of God as a Being whose heart can be pained by our sin flies in the face of the concept of God as a static, abstract, unconcerned idea or as an inflexible principle. It reveals Him as open to the impact of human sin, as a living God touched by what is going on among His human creatures.

Few human beings reflect upon the deep pain that sin inflicts upon God's heart. They think of Him as untouched by our despair. But the biblical picture reveals Him in a different way. It shows Him deeply involved when it comes to sin—not in the sense, certainly, that God Himself is sinful but, rather, in the sense that He responds with deep grief when human beings sin.

This insight into God's heart reveals that He does not judge human sin coldly but instead deals with it in such a way as to control it. This kind of action reflects the kind of situation described in Genesis 6:6.

God determined that the massive and sustained spread of sin needed to be checked. Total perversion to the core of man's will and reasoning powers called for drastic action. That judgment would come in the form of a destructive, worldwide flood that would wipe out "all flesh." God said, "I will blot out man whom I have created from the face of the ground, man and beast and creeping things and birds of the air" (Genesis 6:7, RSV). This passage defines the reference in Genesis 6:13 where God makes the statement, "I have determined to make an end of all flesh; for the earth is filled with violence through them" (RSV). It makes clear that the expression "all flesh" includes "man and beast and creeping things and birds of the air." They had filled the earth with violence or wrong.

God's gracious salvation of the righteous

A number of significant points made in Genesis 6, particularly verses 8 and 9, refer to the salvation of Noah and his family. Three major characteristics of Noah's life contrast vividly against the evil, violence, and corruption of his own generation. First, Noah was a "righteous man" (Genesis 6:9, RSV, NASB, NIV, etc.). His righteousness consisted of the wholeness of his relationship with the Lord. A "righteous person" in the Old Testament does justice to the relationship with God in which he stands. If a person stands in a relationship of faith, trust, and confidence in God, with its resulting obedience to his God, then he is called "righteous."

Second, Noah is designated "blameless" (verse 9, RSV) or "perfect." The words do not connote a state of absolute perfection or sinlessness but one of moral integrity. This totality of commitment gave him a standing without blame before God.

Third, Noah "walked with God" (verse 9). The expression conveys the idea of constancy, undeviating in principle. He is the last member of the antediluvian age and the first of the postdiluvian age to walk with God. As such, he stands as an example of the remnant of faith that survives the cataclysm at the end of time (Hebrews 11:7).

The antediluvian Noachic covenant

We have noted before that the first explicit scriptural reference to God making a covenant appears in Genesis 6:18: "With thee will I establish my covenant; and thou shalt come into the ark, thou, and thy sons, and thy wife, and thy sons' wives with thee." A careful comparison of the wording here with other covenant statements in the Old and New Testaments reveals that it contains the essentials of the biblical covenant. It is definitely a covenant between God and man, God's covenant with Noah.

We find here the covenant partners mentioned, namely, God and man. Always in a biblical covenant God and man relate to each other, with God taking the initiative. Here, too, we find this to be the case.

28

The command "you shall come into the ark" (RSV) reveals that God's covenant with Noah stipulates an obligation. The covenant idea here stands far removed from that of a compact, contract, alliance, bond, or agreement between God and Noah. Indeed, it is *God's* covenant ("my covenant"), and Noah and his family were to be the recipients and the beneficiaries of the covenant blessing resulting from their obedience.

The statement in Genesis 6:18, though brief, contains profound concepts. It predicts provisions for the future of humankind. In establishing this covenant with the one to survive the Flood with his family, God dispenses His bountiful grace and mercy. Humankind's security in the present and assurance of salvation in the future arise out of God's grace and the divine action on their behalf. God shows Himself to be a merciful and a gracious God, steadfast in His love for humanity.

The typical expression for the making of a covenant does not appear in this passage, namely, the one employed in eighty Old Testament instances—"to cut a covenant," or in the typical and appropriate idiomatic expression in English, "to make a covenant." Here the term used is *to establish* (*heqîm*). A careful investigation of this term in connection with covenant making reveals the significance of "to maintain" or "to confirm" (compare Deuteronomy 9:5; 27:26; 1 Samuel 15:11; 2 Samuel 7:25; 2 Kings 23:3, 24; etc.). This discovery gives us the impression that God's establishment of His covenant implies a maintaining of a commitment to which God had pledged Himself earlier.

Even though Genesis 6:18 is the earliest reference to a covenant in the Bible, the use of this particular Hebrew term in connection with it implies that God had previously made a covenant with humankind. In this sense, the covenant of God with Noah may be seen as a renewal of His covenant with Adam, to which the Bible points implicitly in Genesis 3:15.

Noah obviously responded in faith and obedience to God's invitation to enter into a covenant with Him by going into the ark. Noah and his family demonstrated the kind of obedience in which obedience issues out of total and complete trust in God, instead of obedience intended to earn merit in the sight of God.

Genesis 9:8–17 describes the postdiluvian covenant that God made with Noah and his family. Its scope includes the animals as well and demonstrates that coverage by God's grace does not necessarily depend upon understanding or obedience on the part of the covenant's beneficiaries. It is important to note that the covenant in Genesis 9:8–17 is the first and only one in the Bible totally universal in scope.

The postdiluvian covenant that God made with Noah is at times described as an unconditional covenant because it does not mention any specific conditions or obligations laid upon human beings. Whether the instructions in the preceding seven verses ought to be thought of as covenant obligations is not totally clear. Some scholars have understood them to be related and have thereby suggested that this covenant is conditional. In any case, even if no explicit obligations are readily observable, it is assumed that they must be implicit, because they are part of all covenants.

In the covenant made with Noah after the Flood, God promised that never again would a flood cause universal destruction of the earth. This promise does not imply, however, that God is bound never to destroy the world again by means other than water. His declared plan is to use a great destructive fire to end all wickedness at the close of this world's history (2 Peter 3:7, 10, 11; Revelation 20:9). This intention in no way contradicts the promise that God made to Noah and his descendants. "God will destroy the wicked from off the earth. But the righteous will be preserved in the midst of these commotions, as Noah was preserved in the ark. God will be their refuge, and under His wings shall they trust."[3]

Only three biblical covenants include explicit covenant signs. In the postdiluvian Noachic covenant, it is the sign of the rainbow (Genesis 9:12, 13), produced by the refraction of the sun's light through raindrops.

Inasmuch as biblical signs serve important functions, it is important to understand the nature of the sign joined to this covenant. By definition, signs point to something beyond themselves, providing a pledge or guarantee. They may impart knowledge, serve for protection, produce faith, or bring to remembrance and confirm.

Most of these aspects show up in the sign of the rainbow. In contrast to the other two covenant signs (which will be discussed later), the rainbow is an external, physical sign in the clouds that reminds the Lord of His covenant (verses 15, 16) to never again destroy the earth with a flood. Although the rainbow reminds us that God once punished wickedness by a worldwide flood, it guarantees that when clouds bring rain, we need not fear another deluge. It reminds us that God has kept and will keep His promise to never again bring a flood to destroy the earth. The rainbow as a reminder of God's faithfulness to His promise should elicit faithfulness in us and serve as a potent deterrent to a life of sin.

Covenant and the remnant of faith

Few people realize that the first explicit mention of a remnant in the Bible occurs in Genesis 7:23, "Only Noah was left, and those that were with him in the ark" (RSV).[4] The word translated "was left" derives from the Hebrew root šā'ar, of which different forms express the remnant idea in the Old Testament.

In contrast with this explicit reference, an implicit reference to a remnant occurs earlier in the Old Testament within the narrative of the first murder. After Abel had been slain, only Cain was left as the progenitor of the human race until other sons would be born to Adam and Eve (Genesis 4:1–15). Significantly and understandably, Cain is not referred to as a remnant because he is not an example of a remnant of faith, which is a recurring theme in the Old Testament. Contrasting with the reference to a literal remnant in the case of Cain, the reference to a faithful remnant in Genesis 7:23 is more significant. Noah and his family survived the Flood and became the carriers of life for the future of all of humankind. Through them also all the blessings of life came to postdiluvian humankind.

We cannot overlook the fact that the remnant who survived the first

31

worldwide catastrophe were people of faith and trust (Genesis 6:9 and 7:1). Because the Bible used the Noachic Flood as a type of the end-time destruction, this observation has much significance. It is also important to recognize that at the end, the remnant who will be saved will again be people who respond to God by faith and obedience. It will be a remnant who, like Noah, stand in the right relationship with God, a remnant perfect in its sphere, a remnant who walk with God (Revelation 12:17).

Who will belong to the remnant at the end time? Will you qualify as a member?

---

1. For an extensive treatment on the doctrine of sin, see John M. Fowler, "Sin" in *Handbook of Seventh-day Adventist Theology*, Commentary Reference Series, vol. 12 (Hagerstown, MD: Review and Herald®, 2000), 233–270.

2. F. D. Nichols, ed., *Seventh-day Adventist Bible Commentary*, vol. 1 (Washington, DC: Review and Herald®, 1978), 251.

3. Ellen G. White, *Patriarchs and Prophets* (Mountain View, CA: Pacific Press®, 1958), 110.

4. On the concept of the remnant, see Gerhard F. Hasel, *The Remnant: The History and Theology of the Remnant Idea from Genesis to Isaiah*, 2nd ed. (Berrien Springs, MI: Andrews University Press, 1975); Hasel, "Remnant," *Interpreter's Dictionary of the Bible*, supp. vol. (Nashville: Abingdon, 1976), 735–736. Clifford Goldstein, *The Remnant: Biblical Reality or Wishful Thinking?* (Boise, ID: Pacific Press, 1994).

Four

Abrahamic Covenant

When the word of God came to Abraham at Ur of the Chaldees to go to a place that He would show him, Abraham had no idea where he was going (Hebrews 11:8, 9). He had no access to a travel agent who would book a flight. He could not access the internet for a picture gallery of the land of Canaan. Yet, as we will see, the Abrahamic covenant was a covenant of grace and salvation. God initiated it out of His free love (Genesis 12:1, 2; 15:7, 18; 17:1, 2, 7). He revealed Himself to Abraham repeatedly as Yahweh (Genesis 12:1; 15:7). He said, "I am your shield" (Genesis 15:1, RSV), and "I am the Almighty God" (Genesis 17:1). This becomes more significant as we understand where Abraham came from and during which time he lived.[1]

During the early third millennium BC, the city of Ur was the capital of a vast empire. During the reign of its king Ur-nammu, the city experienced a sort of renaissance. Excavations by the British revealed incredible architectural wonders such as the ziggurat—a temple tower that reached into the heavens. The royal cemetery produced the kind of wealth every archaeologist could only dream of finding.[2] Why would God call Abraham out of such a splendid, opulent city? Certainly Abraham did not know. All he had was the promise of God. It was important first for Abraham to know who God was.

The God of the Abrahamic covenant

God engages in an act of self-identification in His address to Abraham in Genesis 15:7, "I am the LORD." When, in English translation, the word *LORD* is printed in capital letters, it means that the Hebrew word was *Yahweh*—a proper noun or personal name of God. Another name, *Elohim,* normally translated into English as *God,* is the generic name for God, in contrast to the personal name Yahweh.

The identification of Yahweh as the One who brought Abraham out of Ur (verse 7) refers back to the initiation of God's covenant with Abraham reported in Genesis 12:1–3. God made a three-stage covenant with Abraham. The first is reported in Genesis 12:1–3; the second in Genesis 15:1–21; and the third in Genesis 17:1–14. Chronological information in the narrative reveals that God engaged in this three-part covenant-making process with Abraham during a twenty-four-year period.

The exact meaning of the name Yahweh cannot be easily established. Entire books have been written on the subject.[3] But in Exodus 3:14 God Himself explains this name to mean "I AM WHO I AM" (RSV, NASB). This unique phrase expresses the reality of God's unconditioned existence and His sovereignty over past, present, and future. In Him reside the initiatives in both creation and salvation and also the ultimate control over the present and the future.

When Abraham was ninety-nine years old, Yahweh appeared to Abraham again and introduced Himself by the divine self-identification of "Almighty God" (Genesis 17:1). This designation (or simply "Almighty") is found principally in two books of the Old Testament: Genesis and Job.

The designation "Almighty God" translates into English the Hebrew *El Shaddai. El* is the generic Semitic name for deity and is used for the most part in the Old Testament as a synonym for Yahweh. Examples of this use are found in Numbers 23:8, 19, 22, 23; 24:4, 8, 16, 23; Psalms 16:1; 17:6; 85:8; Isaiah 40:18; and 42:5. The exact origin and meaning of the name *Shaddai* is not certain. The translation

"Almighty" in the King James Version, as well as RSV and NASB, seems most nearly correct (compare Isaiah 13:6; Joel 1:15). The emphasis on God's "might" over against human frailty admirably fits the experience of Abraham.

God had promised to Abraham a son almost a quarter of a century before the events recorded in Genesis 17. But when he and Sarah still had no son after ten years, Abraham took things into his own hands, married his wife's servant, Hagar, and fathered Ishmael. Almost a decade and a half later, when Abraham had reached the advanced age of ninety-nine, God reaffirmed His covenant and announced to him that it would be established with the birth of a son, Isaac, to be born within a year (Genesis 17:21). At this crucial point, God introduced Himself to Abraham as "Almighty God," for whom nothing is impossible. Hard-pressed men and women, wavering in faith as did Abraham, may be fully reassured that the covenant God is truly an "Almighty God" who brings about the fulfillment of His covenant promises in His own time and without human assistance. What God has promised He is able to perform at any time.

Abraham, partner of God's covenant

God's choice of Abraham was not based on any inherent superiority that called for a reward. Surely Abraham was "faithful among the faithless, uncorrupted by the prevailing apostasy," one who "steadfastly adhered to the worship of the one true God."[4] But his faithfulness must not be construed as merit that earned him the right to be chosen by God. God's choice is always grounded in divine love, grace, and mercy (Deuteronomy 7:6–11).

The biblical record of Abraham's experience reveals a number of actions totally unworthy of one chosen to become a partner in God's covenant (compare Genesis 12:10–20; 16:1–16; 10:1–18). Yet Abraham's pilgrimage reveals a constant growth and advancement that reached heights of faith virtually unparalleled in human history (Genesis 18:22–33; 22:1–14).

At the conclusion of covenant making, God gave Abraham a new name, changed from Abram, meaning "father is exalted," to Abraham, "father of a multitude"—the first person mentioned in the Bible to receive a new name from God. The new name indicated that the new covenant relationship was sealed and the divine promise made certain: "I have made you the father of a multitude of nations" (Genesis 17:5, RSV).

By calling Abraham out of Ur, God not only fulfilled His promise to Abraham that he would be a father of many nations—but He also placed Abraham in a location where this new people would have maximum impact. As a land bridge between empires, Canaan was the natural geographical choice for the people of God. From Canaan they would interact with the Egyptians; the various Canaanite nations—Ammon, Moab, Edom; and the Mesopotamian kingdoms to the east. But there was perhaps a more personal reason why God called Abraham and his family from Ur at that time. Little did Abraham know when he left Ur at the end of the third millennium BC that its prominence as the capital of a flourishing empire would be short-lived. The Ur III period came to an end in 2004/2003 BC, when the city was destroyed by the Elamites.[5] It appears that God not only desired to establish a great nation through the seed of Abraham but He also personally sought to bring Abraham out of a city that would soon meet its demise.

Conditional or unconditional covenant?

Whether the Abrahamic covenant is conditional or unconditional is a matter of heated debate among Christians today. One line of theological interpretation, designated as Dispensationalism, places considerable emphasis on the supposed unconditionality of the Abrahamic covenant. The *New Scofield Bible* suggests that the Abrahamic covenant reveals the sovereign purpose of God to fulfill through Abraham His program for Israel and to provide the Savior for all who believe. Further, it asserts that the ultimate fulfillment is made to rest upon the divine promise and the power of God rather than upon human faithfulness.[6]

Dispensationalist interpreters argue that just as the promises to physical Israel were unconditional, so also are the promises to the families of the earth who will bless themselves in Abraham. *The New Scofield Bible* states that "the new covenant [in which Gentiles participate] . . . secures the eternal blessedness, under the Abrahamic Covenant, of all who believe. It is absolutely unconditional and, since no responsibility is by it committed to man, it is final and irreversible."[7] Based on this interpretation of the covenant made with Abraham, many modern-day Christians claim that the state of Israel formed in 1948 fulfills the promise God made to Abraham in Genesis 12:1–13 and succeeding passages. They also believe, therefore, that the state of Israel will play a major role as a nation in the concluding work of God on earth.

Many other Christians, on the other hand, have found significant difficulties with the interpretation of the Abrahamic covenant as an unconditional covenant.[8] In the book *Patriarchs and Prophets,* Ellen G. White notes, "By this rite [circumcision] they [Abraham's descendants] were pledged to fulfill, on their part, the conditions of the covenant made with Abraham."[9]

The book of Genesis provides evidence to support this view. In an explicit statement, God charges Abraham and his seed after him to "keep" (in Hebrew *šmar*) the covenant that God made with them (Genesis 17:9). The same word is the term used for the keeping of subsequent Old Testament covenants. For example, the covenant God made with Moses, recognized by all to be a conditional covenant, had to be "kept" (Deuteronomy 29:9). The same term *keep* appears more than thirty times in the book of Deuteronomy for the keeping of commandments (see, for example, Deuteronomy 4:2). In various parts of the Scripture, it is also employed specifically for the keeping of the Sabbath (Exodus 31:13, 14, 16; Deuteronomy 5:12; etc.) as well as of certain feasts (Exodus 13:10; 23:15; 34:18).

In the same chapter of Genesis, we also find that the Abrahamic covenant can indeed be "broken" (Hebrew, *pārar*; Genesis 17:14). It is remarkable that this same Hebrew word appears frequently, exactly twenty-two times, in the Old Testament as a typical term for the idea of the breaking of the covenant (Leviticus 26:15; Deuteronomy 31:16, 20; Isaiah 24:5; etc). Evidently Abraham's covenant, according to this covenant chapter in the early part of the Abrahamic story, can be either kept or broken by the human partners concerned, obviously making it a conditional covenant.

Other explicit statements in Genesis also indicate that the Abrahamic covenant is conditional in that it required the one with whom the covenant was made to be faithful to the Lord. Genesis 18:18, 19 states: "Abraham shall become a great and mighty nation, and all the nations of the earth shall bless themselves by him. . . . I have chosen him, that he may charge his children and his household after him to keep the way of the LORD by doing righteousness and justice; so that the LORD may bring to Abraham what he has promised him" (RSV). Abraham was to train his family and household in the way of the Lord, so that when he died, his descendants would live as he had lived. Abraham's descendants would also have "to keep the way of the Lord," in order for the Lord to "bring to Abraham what he has promised him."

Abraham's faith response is manifested in his obedience to God's instructions, paramountly in his willingness to sacrifice Isaac—a submissive attitude that keeps the promise effective. A study of Genesis 22:16– 18 is particularly important in this connection. Abraham becomes the model of all who are justified by faith (Genesis 15:6; see Romans 4) and demonstrates that justifying faith is always accompanied by obedience to God's law (Genesis 26:5).

The covenant sign of circumcision

Just as the Noachic covenant was accompanied by a sign, so also was the Abrahamic covenant. The sign of God's covenant with Abraham was circumcision. God calls it a "sign of the covenant between me and you" (Genesis 17:11, RSV).

This covenant sign communicated several significant truths. First, it distinguished Abraham's descendants from the Gentiles (Ephesians 2:11). Second, it perpetuated the memory of God's covenant (Genesis

17:11) and symbolized a circumcision of the heart; and, third, it fostered the cultivation of moral purity (Deuteronomy 10:16; Romans 2:29). Fourth, it represented the righteousness that comes by faith (Romans 4:11). Fifth, it foreshadowed the Christian ordinance of baptism (Colossians 2:11, 12).

A few years ago an eighteen-year-old man immigrated to the modern state of Israel. Because his mother was a Jew, he was eligible for citizenship. As part of becoming a citizen of Israel, he was required by law to become circumcised—a rather painful prospect for an adult! Some may wonder whether circumcision is still a valid sign for God's people. It would be best to answer this question from the viewpoint of the New Testament. The apostle Paul defines circumcision in the following way: "Real circumcision is a matter of the heart, spiritual and not literal" (Romans 2:29, RSV). The New Testament insists that for the believer, neither physical circumcision nor uncircumcision count for anything (1 Corinthians 7:19). It does emphasize, however, that "faith working through love" (Galatians 5:6, RSV), becoming "a new creation" (Galatians 6:15, RSV), and "keeping the commandments of God" (1 Corinthians 7:19, RSV) continue to have significance today.

---

1. The early chronology of Abraham is adopted here, dating Abraham's journey from Ur at 2092 BC, see J. J. Bimson, "Archaeological Data and the Dating of the Patriarchs," in *Essays on the Patriarchal Narratives*, eds. A. R. Millard and D. J. Wiseman (Winona Lake, IN: Eisenbrauns, 1980), 53–89.

2. Susan Pollack, "Ur," in *The Oxford Encyclopedia of Archaeology in the Near East*, ed. E. M. Meyers (New York: Oxford University Press, 1997), 288–291; cf. excavation reports by C. Leonard Woolley, *Ur of the Chaldees* (Ithica, NY: Cornell University Press, 1982).

3. G. H. Parke-Taylor, *Yahweh: The Divine Name in the Bible* (Waterloo, ON: Wilfred Laurier University Press, 1975); Millard C. Lind, *Yahweh Is a Warrior* (Scottdale, PA: Herald Press, 1980).

4. Ellen G. White, *Patriarchs and Prophets* (Mountain View, CA: Pacific Press®, 1958), 125.

5. Jean-Claude Margueron, "Ur," in *Anchor Bible Dictionary*, vol. 6, ed. D. N. Freedman (New York: Doubleday, 1992), 766, 767; C. E. Carter, "A Brief History of the Third Dynasty of Ur," *Biblical Archaeologist* 50/3 (1987): 141–143.

6. C. I. Scofield, ed., *The New Scofield Bible* (Oxford: Oxford University Press, 1967), 20.

7. Scofield, *The New Scofield Bible*, 1318.

8. Bruce K. Waltke, "The Phenomenon of Conditionality Within Unconditional Covenants," in *Israel's Apostasy and Restoration: Essays in Honor of Roland K. Harrison*, ed. Abraham Gileadi (Grand Rapids, MI: Baker Book House, 1988), 123–139; Ronald Youngblood, "The Abrahamic Covenant: Conditional or Unconditional?" in *The Living and Active Word of God: Studies in Honor of Samuel J. Schultz*, eds. Morris Inch and Ronald Youngblood (Winona Lake, IN: Eisenbrauns, 1983), 31–46.

9. White, *Patriarchs and Prophets*, 138.

Five

Divine Promise and the Abrahamic Covenant

The divine promise weaves itself through the Bible as a scarlet thread. It constitutes the theme, some suggest, that unites the first five books of the Bible. Other theologians go even further, suggesting that divine promise is the key biblical theme that unites both the Old and the New Testaments.[1]

It may be hard to sustain such all-inclusive claims, but it is certain that to the helpless, the suffering, and everyone else who walk the path of faith, the promises of God are like leaves from the tree of life. When personalized, God's promises comfort the soul and provide a foundation for faith: "Make the promises of God your own, Then when test and trial come, these promises will be to you glad springs of heavenly comfort."[2]

God's promises stand in contrast to human promises. Human promises have the earmarks of those who make them and are subject to human frailty. In this chapter, we are not speaking of the kind of promise that Jacob exacted from Joseph—that he be taken out of Egypt and buried in the land of his fathers (Genesis 47:29–31). Nor are we talking about the kind of promise that Moses commanded the Israelites to keep (Deuteronomy 23:23; Numbers 32:24). And we certainly are not talking about promises such as Balak made to Balaam and Haman made to King

Ahasuerus—promises motivated by evil intentions (Numbers 22:17; Esther 4:7). The kind of promises we are talking about are different, as the succeeding pages will emphasize—namely, the promises of God.

Divine promises

God made many promises recorded throughout the Bible. He made promises at different times and in different circumstances. God made promises that relate to preservation, protection, posterity, possessions, and prosperity—earthly matters. He also made promises that relate to spiritual matters. One such promise is Genesis 3:15, which has far-reaching implications. In it God announced the plan of salvation and how it would be worked out through the seed (Jesus Christ), crushing the head of the serpent (Satan). It included a promise that enmity would exist between the seed of the woman and the seed of the serpent; that is, enmity between the two strands of humankind—the believing and the unbelieving.

Because the concept of promise is so prominent in both the Old and New Testaments, it is important to recognize that it is God's word that makes the promise sure. God Himself is speaking, making Himself responsible for the support of His people and for their destiny.

The promises that God made to Abraham are among the most profound in the Bible because they are associated with God's covenant with Abraham. They relate to God's constant presence with His servant, assuring Abraham that God would be a "shield" to him. God also gave a Messianic promise to be fulfilled through the seed of Abraham. He promised to make Abraham a great and mighty nation. God also promised to make the name of Abraham great. And furthermore, He promised to give him and his offspring a land of their own. We will focus on these promises in more detail.

The God of covenantal promise

Among God's acts of self-revelation are those in which He engages in a self-presentation. God presented Himself to Abraham as Yahweh (see

Genesis 12:1; 15:7). We have already seen that this name, Yahweh, is God's personal name and is also a designation of the covenant God. We also have noted that God has presented Himself to Abraham as "Almighty God" (Genesis 17:1). We have seen that in presenting Himself as the "Almighty," He gave assurance that He is powerful, infinitely capable of fulfilling the divine promise.

But God not only revealed Himself to Abraham as Yahweh and as Almighty God, He also addressed him with a personal greeting of encouragement, "Fear not" (Genesis 15:1). How timely this greeting—and how appropriate! Abraham's mind had become "so oppressed by forebodings that he could not now grasp the promise with unquestioning confidence as heretofore. . . . How was the covenant to be realized," he questioned, "while the gift of a son was withheld?"[3]

Abraham at this time had no natural son. Should he continue to trust the Lord and believe His promise even though he was of advanced age? Or should he follow the custom of his time and provide an heir for himself? Should he take things into his own hands and assist God in fulfilling His promise? According to Genesis 15:1–6, we learn that Abraham opted for the established custom of his time and planned to adopt Eliezer of Damascus as his legal heir.

According to archaeological findings, at that time a person without an heir could legally adopt one. This legal heir would have all the privileges and property rights, as well as the responsibilities, of a normal heir or son. At this particular moment Abraham had decided to move in the direction of adoption, but God appeared to him in a vision and assured him, "I am your shield" (Genesis 15:1, RSV).

Please note the personal pronoun "your" in God's promise. God says to Abraham, "I am your shield." This pronoun *your* reveals the intimate interest God takes in the affairs of the one whose faith is wavering and is being tested.

The designation of God as "shield" appears here for the first time in the Bible, and it is the only time it appears as a self-revelation of God. Later, the same expression is repeatedly used when individuals speak about God (see Deuteronomy 33:29; Psalms 18:2, 30; 84:11; 144:2).

God is the "shield" of Abraham, the man of faith. God is every believer's "shield"; that is, his or her protection. The "shield" or protection spoken of here does not refer to physical protection in war or physical protection from misfortune. Rather, it refers to protection from the possibility that the covenant promise would not be fulfilled through Abraham and his future seed. God's promise to Abraham that He would be his shield is the same promise made to every descendant of Abraham. If we are Abraham's seed (and all who have the faith of Abraham are Abraham's seed), then we also have the assurance that God will be our shield. God will shield us in every aspect of our lives—but especially in the sense that He will fulfill the great promise that has not yet come to pass.

The promise of divine presence

The promise of the risen Christ before His ascension was, "Lo, I am with you alway, even unto the end of the world" (Matthew 28:20). This promise of Jesus Christ given to all His disciples, not to those present at the Ascension alone, is one of the great themes of the Bible. Few people realize that this pre-Ascension promise simply reiterates similar and oft-repeated promises throughout the Old Testament.

The promise of God's continuing presence and His intimate companionship, expressed by the phrases "I am with you" or "I will be with you" (Genesis 26:3, 4; 28:15; 31:3; Exodus 3:12; Deuteronomy 31:23; Joshua 1:9; 3:7; 7:12; Isaiah 41:10; Jeremiah 1:8; Haggai 1:13; etc.), is one of the prominent themes of the Bible. In many instances this promise of God's presence is connected with the charge, "Fear not!" (Deuteronomy 20:1; 31:8; Isaiah 41:10; 43:5; etc.).

The promise of a blessing for all families

God gave another covenantal promise with immense future potential, the promise made to Abraham in Genesis 12:3, "In thee shall all families of the earth be blessed." He repeated this promise in Genesis 28:14—"In thee and in thy seed shall all the families of the earth be blessed"—here exploding all narrow, nationalistic expectations that any follower of Abraham or any of his descendants might have. The horizons of this promise are expansive, its dimensions universal. The scope of the blessing is all-inclusive. Its benefits are totally unrestricted.

Some modern translations render the words "be blessed" in Genesis 12:3 in the reflexive way as "bless themselves." We will not attempt to discuss the complexities of the Hebrew verbal forms used in Genesis 12:3; 18:18; 26:4; and 28:14. We may suggest, however, that solid linguistic grounds support the translation "will be blessed" as expressing the original intention of the text.

The apostle Paul builds a forceful argument on the singular use of the word "seed" when writing to the believers in Galatia. In Galatians 3:8, 16, he demonstrates that the intent of the singular word was met by none other than Jesus Christ Himself.

We find in the second sermon that the apostle Peter preached, recorded in Acts 3, a reference back to Genesis 12:3 and 22:18, where Peter also applies the seed to God's servant, Jesus Christ. Obviously both Peter and Paul recognized in this promise an intended Messianic application. Paul further clarified that literal physical descent from Abraham provided no guarantee of a spiritual relationship, which is by faith and not by ethnic descent. This good news for the believer is summarized in Galatians 3:29 (RSV): "If you are Christ's, then you are Abraham's offspring, heirs according to promise."

The divine promise of a great nation

In a number of instances within the framework of the Abrahamic covenant, God made the covenantal promise that Abraham would become a great nation. We find it first communicated to Abraham in Genesis 12:2, "I will make of you a great nation" (RSV). It is repeated later on to Abraham in a statement found in Genesis 18:18, "Abraham will surely become a great and mighty nation" (NASB). At the time when Abraham was without offspring, the God in whom he trusted made the covenant promise that not only would He give him a son and posterity

(Genesis 12:7; 13:15; 15:18; 17:16, 19, 30, etc.), but He also would make Abraham a great and mighty nation.

Before Jacob moved from the Promised Land, Canaan, to Egypt, God repeated to him the promise initially made to his grandfather, Abraham: "I will there [in Egypt] make of you a great nation" (Genesis 46:3, RSV). These words not only restate the promise originally made to Abraham but also assure Jacob that God will fulfill the promise in a particular place, namely, in Egypt. God achieves His purposes in His own way, in His own time, and in His own place. When Jacob was few in number (Genesis 46:8–27), only seventy people, they moved to Egypt. From that small and seemingly insignificant number, the descendants of Jacob increased and became so populous that they developed into a great nation (Deuteronomy 26:5). In Egypt, Israel had no land of its own and no prospect of acquiring any. Yet in God's miraculous way, Israel became a "nation." So God fulfilled in a spectacular way the promise of Abraham's descendents becoming a great nation.

In terms of population alone, Israel indeed became a "nation" in Egypt. But in terms of a cohesive religious community, Israel became a nation only later, when they entered into a formative and binding relationship, the covenantal relationship, with their Lord at Mount Sinai. At that point in their experience, when they became a covenant people, they were to function as a "holy nation" (Exodus 19:6), totally set apart to serve their God, to worship Him, and to be of service to others.

The divine promise of a great name

A typical human pursuit is to attempt to make a name for oneself, to gain reputation and fame, to become a celebrity. In the annals of secular history we find this story of aspiration and endeavor time and again. The Bible also includes accounts of this focus on fame, one extremely crucial for the human race.

The builders of the Tower of Babel, according to Genesis 11:1–9, were seeking to make a name for themselves. So they said to one another, "Let us make a name for ourselves" (Genesis 11:4, RSV). But as typically happens to people motivated by selfish aims, the builders of the Tower of Babel failed miserably in their driving ambition to make an illustrious name for themselves.

The contrast between what the builders of the Tower of Babel attempted and what God would accomplish for Abraham is vivid and arresting. On the one hand, the entire human race joined together to make a name for itself and ended up in such monumental failure and confusion that the results still plague us today. On the other hand, one lone person, Abraham, a man who trusted in God and lived in faith and obedience to his Lord, entered into a covenant relationship with God. To him God promised, "I will bless you, and make your name great" (Genesis 12:2, RSV). And because Abraham responded to God's terms, God Himself pledged to bequeath to this one man what others so selfishly sought and failed to attain. Likewise God, by His grace, does for anyone who enters into covenant relationship with Him what no person can ever do for him or herself—to make for that person a great name as God defines greatness.

The divine promise of the land

Another promise of great importance that God gave to Abraham was that he should have a land that the Lord would show him: "Go from your country . . . to the land that I will show you" (Genesis 12:1, RSV). Notice the significant contrast between "your country," on the one hand, and "the land I will show you," on the other. In other words, in the command to leave one land and go to another, as God would direct, rested the plan that God had for Abraham and the fulfillment of the promise to inherit Canaan that He intended for him to enjoy.

Once Abraham had entered the Land of Canaan, the Promised Land, the Lord appeared to him again and made it clear that while Abraham himself was only to sojourn in the Land of Canaan, the land would eventually be given to his seed as a possession (Genesis 12:7). This promise was repeated to Abraham again after he and Lot had separated (Genesis 13:14, 15, 17). It was repeated also in the experience of covenant ratification recorded in Genesis 15. Then in the final phase of covenant making recorded in Genesis 17:8, the promise was repeated still another time. Even after these assurances, God continued to repeat the promise to Abraham's son Isaac (Genesis 26:2–5) and to Isaac's son Jacob (Genesis 28:13, 15 and 35:12).

God revealed to Abraham in Genesis 15:13, 16 that the fulfillment of the promise would come 400 years later. After four centuries, the Lord announced to Moses that He would bring the children of Israel out of the land of Egypt into a good and spacious land, a land flowing with milk and honey (Exodus 3:8, 17; 6:8). So it was during the time of Moses that the promise began at last to meet its fulfillment. Yet Moses himself was not allowed to enter the Promised Land. He would see the better land of the heavenly world instead. God reiterated the promise to Joshua (Joshua 1:3), when he led the people into Canaan. In David's day the promise had finally reached its fulfillment, though not completely even then (see Genesis 15:18–21; 2 Samuel 8:1–14; 10; 1 Chronicles 19; 1 Kings 4:21). It had taken a long time for the promise to be realized.

The Lord of the covenant is a God of promise. His promises are secured in His Being. God's promises are certain. He fulfills His promises in His own time and in the way He intends. Trusting in God and His Word of promise and submitting to the terms of the covenant make us part of the experience of promise and part of the people of promise who will someday occupy the true Land of Promise with the Lord.

---

1. Walter C. Kaiser Jr., "The Centre of Old Testament Theology: The Promise," *Themelios* 10 (1974): 1–10; Kaiser, *Toward an Old Testament Theology* (Grand Rapids, MI: Zondervan, 1978), 23.

2. Ellen G. White, *My Life Today* (Hagerstown, MD: Review and Herald®, 1980), 28.

3. Ellen G. White, *Patriarchs and Prophets* (Mountain View, CA: Pacific Press®, 1958), 136.

Six

The True Israel and the Promised Land

The modern state of Israel is a land of contrasts. It is a modern industrial nation that boasts some of the most sophisticated technologies ranging from manufacturing pharmaceuticals to developing the latest in flash memory in the world's largest Intel plant. Yet one can also still see Bedouin living in tents and moving from place to place, living not much differently from the way Abraham did nearly four thousand years ago. It is land of religious diversity containing the sacred holy sites of Judaism, Christianity, and Islam. One can see Muslims praying while facing Mecca, then later see them bargaining in the street markets of the Old City. One is struck by the contrast of Hasidic Jews bowing rhythmically in prayer at the Western Wall on Sabbath while Jewish young people dance to a rock band near Ben Yahuda Street on Saturday night.

Indeed the name "Israel" itself brings various and frequently conflicting ideas to mind. Many think of the state of Israel established on May 14, 1948, under the auspices of the United Nations. Others imagine the Israel of the Bible, the people of God who lived long ago. Christians may think of the church, as certain passages in the New Testament would prompt them to. Dispensationalists might also think of an Israel of God of the future—a people whom they believe will reign for a thousand years on earth.

Whether we think of Israel of the past or Israel of the present or Israel of the future, the burning question remains, Who constitute the true "Israel of God"? Only the blood descendants of Abraham? Exclusively those who hold citizenship in the state of Israel today? A combination of Jews and Christians? The composite Christian church? Who belongs to the true Israel? Do you belong to the true Israel?

The making of Israel

We, understandably, must begin our investigation in the Old Testament. There, from the way God describes His purpose for Israel of old, we may understand how the concept of Israel originally came into existence and what the concept includes. First of all, we have to recognize that the Israel of Old Testament times became a national entity because God chose it to be His "holy people" (Deuteronomy 7:6; 14:2; 26:18, 19). In one instance, and in one alone, God designated Israel as a "holy nation" (Exodus 19:6).

God's expressed design that the Israel He established in Egypt should be a "holy people" or a "holy nation" clearly indicates that it was His own initiative to make them "holy." This observation clarifies that Israel of old, designated by the names "holy people" or "holy nation," was not characterized by an inherent holiness that made them worthy of merit. Rather, the term "holy" expressed the divine choice that separated this people, or cut them off from other peoples as well as from pagan practices, to fulfill a specific purpose in God's plan for the salvation of the world.

Of special significance is the fact that Israel was to be a "kingdom of priests" and a "holy nation" (Exodus 19:5, 6). The expression "kingdom of priests" is not a synonym for "holy nation," nor can it be reduced to the idea of their being royal priests or priest-kings. The covenantal setting on Mount Sinai (see Exodus 19), during which God conferred this title on them, reveals that the expression "kingdom of priests" designated

50

Israel as a covenant people. This covenant people was to have its purpose among surrounding earthly nations and states—but not simply as another nation or state alongside them. Rather, God designed that they, as a priestly kingdom, would do service among and for the nations of the world, a kingdom of priests functioning within society at large to reveal God and His way of life to them.

The expression "holy nation" (Exodus 19:6) continues to emphasize this special role God had in mind for Israel. The idea of being "holy" contained nothing of an inherent superior status. Instead, it expressed that Israel had been separated or set apart from the other nations by God's grace for a specific purpose. It was set apart to belong to God and to reveal in the quality of its total life and existence the covenant relationship into which God had placed it—and to lead others into the same relationship. Whenever this chosen people failed to meet God's ideal for them, Israel no longer remained the true Israel of God but was reduced to the level of an ordinary political-national entity.

The promise of the land

In the previous chapter, we have investigated the promise of the land, as recorded in Genesis 12:1–3. We have seen how in unquestioning obedience Abraham left Ur (Genesis 11:31) and subsequently Haran "to go into the land of Canaan" (Genesis 12:4, 5). Once Abraham had arrived in the land of Canaan, the Lord appeared to him in Shechem and promised him, "To your descendants I will give this land" (Genesis 12:7, RSV). What is this land? What is its territorial extent?

We don't have to search very far in the book of Genesis to find that God revealed to Abraham the territorial extent of the land promised to him. In Genesis 15:18–21 we have a brief outline of it: the Euphrates River on the northeast, the entrance of Hamath to the north, the "Great Sea" or Mediterranean Sea on the west, the River of Egypt (Nile) on the south, and the wilderness on the east. The territorial extent of the land promised later to Moses was essentially identical (see Exodus 23:31; Deuteronomy 11:24; compare Joshua 1:4).

God made it clear that the promise of the land was conditional. "If in spite of this, you do not obey Me," He said, "I will make the land desolate. . . . You, however, I will scatter among the nations" (Leviticus 26:27, 32, 33, NASB). Disobedience would bring loss of the land promised to literal Israel.

In this connection, we also will have to recall statements from other prophets in various parts of the Old Testament that reveal how God had hoped that Israel would be faithful to Him but in reality they fell into obstinate disobedience. Instead of being dedicated and separated as a "kingdom of priests" and a "holy nation," they became a "people laden with iniquity" (Isaiah 1:4, RSV). Time and again God sent His prophets to call them back; but the people "deeply corrupted themselves" (Hosea 9:9, RSV) and were bent on turning away from God (Hosea 11:7; Amos 3:1; Ezekiel 16:2, 23; etc.).

Time of the fulfillment of the Promised Land

The fulfillment of the promise that Israel would receive the land began during the days of Moses. The book of Exodus recounts clearly the preparations made for their deliverance from Egypt, the deliverance itself, the covenant that God made on Mount Sinai with them, the wilderness wanderings, the instructions for the tabernacle, the apostasy, and the renewal of the covenant. Moses, in his farewell speeches states, "Behold, I have set the land before you; go in and take possession of the land" (Deuteronomy 1:8, RSV).

The death of Moses signaled the imminent conquest of the Promised Land (Joshua 1:1–9). The miraculous crossing of the Jordan provided a visible token of God's constant presence and further evidence that it was His purpose to give them the Promised Land (Joshua 3:1–17). By the time of Joshua's death (Joshua 23:1, 14), the Lord had given to Israel "all the land which he swore to give to their fathers; and having taken possession of it, they settled there. . . . Not one of the good promises which the Lord had made to the house of Israel had failed; all came to pass" (Joshua 21:43–45, RSV; compare Joshua 23:14).

The "remnant of these nations" (Joshua 23:12), still living among the Hebrews, became so powerless that they proved no threat to Israel, so long as Israel adhered faithfully to their God (Joshua 23:11–13). Notwithstanding that parts of the country remained in the hands of pagan peoples (Joshua 13:1–6), the promises had been fulfilled. God had not promised the immediate destruction of all the Canaanites but their gradual extermination (Exodus 23:20, 30; Deuteronomy 7:22). In all of this, the God of Israel acted in a way consistent with His own character.

The failure of Israel
and the conditional promise of restoration

The fulfillment of God's marvelous promises, including the promise of the land, hinged upon Israel's fidelity. "This shall come to pass, if you will diligently obey the voice of the LORD your God" (Zechariah 6:15, RSV). If the Israelites were disobedient, God could not bestow His blessings upon them. God would not only withhold His blessings— but also, in harmony with the covenant stipulations, He would pluck the Israelites from the Promised Land and scatter them among the nations. God never desired to punish His people (Hosea 11:8, 9), but their continued unfaithfulness left Him with no other choice. But even then, He designed that the punishment would teach them lessons of faithfulness and obedience.

In 722 BC, when the city of Samaria fell to the Assyrians, the northern kingdom of Israel experienced the fulfillment of divine threatenings (Deuteronomy 28:63–68; 31:20–22; Leviticus 26:3–33). A century and a half later, the southern kingdom of Judah was plucked up and scattered throughout the Neo-Babylonian Empire (2 Kings 17:7–22).

The exile of ancient Israel did not mean the end of God's plan for His people. God held out hope of restoration and a return to their land. The prophet Isaiah predicted that the Lord would "extend his hand yet a second time to recover the remnant which is left of his people, from Assyria, from Egypt, from Pathros, from Ethiopia, from Elam, from Shinar, from Hamath, and from the coastlands of the sea . . . and gather the dispersed of Judah from the four corners of the earth" (Isaiah 11:11, 12, RSV).

This promise envisions the recovery of only a "remnant" from Israel, in contrast to the earlier recovery of *all* Israel from Egyptian slavery. The expression "second time" did not imply a gathering in the distant future—a gathering similar to the return of Jews to the present state of Israel—because the countries and places mentioned are all territories where the ancient Israelites were taken in the Assyrian and Babylonian captivities. The phrase "four corners of the earth" means the four directions of the compass, corresponding to the territories included in verse 11. Thus the second gathering to which Isaiah refers was the one that took place in Persian times. That prophecy met its fulfillment in the return of the exiles, as recorded in the book of Ezra.

It does not come as a surprise that the prophet Jeremiah, who ministered during the last years of the kingdom of Judah, presented a distinct message of the divine restoration of his people. "They shall dwell in their own land," he assured them (Jeremiah 23:8). Promising to "restore their fortunes" (Jeremiah 32:44, RSV), the Lord refers back to the promise He had made to the patriarchs: "I will let you dwell in this place, in the land that I gave of old to your fathers for ever" (Jeremiah 7:7, RSV). These promises of return and restoration are based upon the covenant relationship: "I will be your God, and you shall be my people" (see Jeremiah 7:23; 11:4; 24:7; 30:22; 31:33; 32:38). This correlation must be seen as background as we study Israel's failure, already outlined in detail by Isaiah (Isaiah 40:2; 42:24; 50:1; 54:7, 8), who also emphasizes the results that could take place from a reestablishment of a genuine covenant relationship with God (Isaiah 55:3–5; 54:9, 10; 42:6; 49:8).

The constant interrelationship between restoration in the physical sense *and* restoration of the people's inner lives is also maintained by Jeremiah. Without the inner restoration, based on the new covenant "within them," with the law written "upon their hearts" (Jeremiah 31:31–34, RSV), there can be no genuine restoration in the physical sense. The new covenant will make a new people. Repentance was to be the condition for receiving and remaining in possession of the Promised Land. "Amend your ways and your doings, and I will let you dwell in this place" (Jeremiah 7:3 RSV; compare Jeremiah 18:11; 22:3–5). The numerous promises of restoration in Jeremiah (Jeremiah 23:1–8; 24:4–7; 30:8, 9, 18–21; 31:27, 28; 32:6–23) and other Old Testament promises are all conditioned by the "ifs" of obedience as well as by the "if nots" of disobedience (Jeremiah 17:24, 27; 18:8–10; 22:5; Zechariah 6:15).

The remnant as true Israel

God's plan for Israel as a religious-political entity was frustrated by Israel's long history of disobedience and unfaithfulness. But God's plan actually was not truly frustrated, because the true Israel, as God continued to reveal it, is an Israel of faith and of obedience. So within the national entity, the national entity of unfaithful Israel, there continued to exist faithful individuals, faithful Israelites. Evidence of this fact comes to light in the case of Elijah and the 7,000 who would not bow their knees to Baal (1 Kings 19:14, 18). Thus Elijah, with those who refused to bow their knees to the idol, constituted the remnant, or the true Israel, the true people of God. They existed within the nation of Israel.

Many of the Old Testament prophets speak of this faithful remnant within the nation of Israel itself. "I will leave in the midst of you a people humble and lowly. They shall seek refuge in the name of the LORD, those who are left in Israel; they shall do no wrong and utter no lies, nor shall there be found in their mouth a deceitful tongue" (Zephaniah 3:12, 13, RSV). Such a true remnant of Israel will have accepted the Lord's rulership (Micah 4:7; compare Micah 2:12, 13). They are a "holy seed" (Isaiah 6:13), a holy remnant recorded for life (Isaiah 4:3). This faithful remnant is a religious entity, not a national one. Possessing "one heart" and a "new spirit" (Ezekiel 11:16–21; compare Jeremiah 31:31–34; Ezekiel 36:26), these faithful ones will live on the basis and terms of the new covenant (Jeremiah 31:31–34).

God's purpose in creating and preserving a faithful remnant within the national-political entity Israel was to make this remnant the carriers of the promises of God and to use them as divinely appointed instruments for declaring God's "glory among the nations" (Isaiah 66:19, RSV). This witness, given universally among "all nations and tongues" (Isaiah 66:18, RSV), would lead others outside Israel to join the faithful to "worship the King, the LORD of hosts" (Zechariah 14:16, RSV). Thus the faithful remnant constitutes the true Israel within an apostate nation of Israel. True Israel is then evidently a spiritual entity, a spiritual Israel, not bound by blood relationship to Abraham. In this sense, we see evidence in the Old Testament that God looked forward to a true, spiritual Israel that would be made up of descendants of Abraham and also of members of the Gentile nations.

The New Testament makes three clear references to "Israel" in which this term is applied to the universal church (Romans 9:4–8; Ephesians 2:11–19; Galatians 6:15, 16). The New Testament clearly argues that mere blood descent from Abraham was never an ironclad guarantee of membership in the true Israel. Paul showed from the Old Testament that "not all who are descended from Israel belong to Israel" (Romans 9:6, RSV). Rather, the true Israel is "a remnant, chosen by grace" (Romans 11:5, RSV). It is a new creation (Galatians 6:15).

Heirs of the promise

The apostle Paul engages in a sustained argument in Galatians 3 and Romans 4 to prove that men and women are saved by faith and that it is "men of faith who are the sons of Abraham" (Galatians 3:7, RSV). The promise of blessing belongs to men and women of faith (Galatians 3:9) and not to those who merely claim a blood relationship with Abraham. Jewish thought at the time of the apostle Paul claimed that Gentiles were to share in the promised blessings made to Abraham, provided they would worship the Lord and submit to circumcision. The apostle Paul, however, insists that Scripture foresaw their share in the blessings promised to Abraham prior to the introduction of circumcision (see Romans 4:9–12).

They may share the blessings promised to Abraham as the offspring or children of Abraham by faith in Jesus Christ. "If you are Christ's, then you are Abraham's offspring, heirs according to promise" (Galatians 3:29, RSV). "All who through Christ should become the children of faith were to be counted as Abraham's seed; they were inheritors of the covenant promises; like Abraham, they were called to guard and make known to the world the law of God and the gospel of His Son."[1]

The apostle Peter, as well as Paul, affirms that the Christian church is not a national group with distinct lineal descent from Abraham but a people called out from every nation, kindred, tongue, and people to constitute one true, spiritual Israel throughout the world. The apostle Peter declares, "You are a chosen people, a royal priesthood, a holy nation, a people belonging to God, that you may declare the praises of him who called you out of darkness into his wonderful light. Once you were not a people, . . . but now you have received mercy" (1 Peter 2:9, 10, NIV). Peter claims that God has assigned to the Christian community the privileges and responsibilities He had wanted literal, physical Israel of old to experience and fulfill.

Peter assigns to the true people of God several titles once assigned to literal Israel of old. First Peter 1:1, 2 and 2:9 echo the expression "chosen people" or "chosen generation" or "chosen race" found in such texts as Isaiah 43:20. These titles emphasize the divine election and express the destiny of the church.

The title "royal priesthood" (1 Peter 2:9) derives from Exodus 19:6, where Israel is said to function in God's plan as "a kingdom of priests" or a priestly kingdom. Israel, because of her disobedience, had forfeited her status as a priestly kingdom; and now the Israel of faith, the church, made up of Jews and Gentiles, is assigned this role. Now the community of believers is to offer to God "spiritual sacrifices" (1 Peter 2:5) and "living sacrifices" (Romans 12:1).

The designation "a holy nation" also is derived from Exodus 19:6. It indicates that the true Israel of God in the form of the believing community, the church, is totally set apart from the world to represent Him on earth.

The fourth title, "a people belonging to God" (1 Peter 2:9, NIV) or, in more traditional language, "a peculiar people," makes clear that God through Christ has acquired and considers this new amalgam of believers His own special possession. Literal Israel, the national-political entity of the past, had been the object of God's particular affection. But now this affection is transferred to the true Israel, the church, which is the community of all believers.[2] All the titles of privilege conferred on Israel of old are assigned to the new Israel of faith, the spiritual Israel, the true Israel, which is the church made up of different races, nations, and peoples. The profound unity manifested in the church as God's race, nation, and people, transcends all barriers and distinctions, whether ethnic, social, economic, or political because it is grounded in Jesus Christ. We are all one in Christ, and we are all one with one another.

---

1. Ellen G. White, *Patriarchs and Prophets* (Mountain View, CA: Pacific Press®, 1958), 476.

2. For a more thorough development of separation between spiritual Israel and literal Israel, see Hans K. LaRondelle, *The Israel of God in Prophecy: Principles of Prophetic Interpretation* (Berrien Springs, MI: Andrews University Press, 1983); Gerhard F. Hasel, "Israel in Bible Prophecy," *Journal of the Adventist Theological Society* 3/1 (1992): 120–155; for a thorough critique of dispensationalist theology, see Samuele Bacchiocchi, *The Advent Hope for Human Hopelessness* (Berrien Springs, MI: Biblical Perspectives, 1986), 214–262.

Seven

Redemption and Covenant at Sinai

We began our journey at 2:00 A.M. in the darkness of night. The desert was now cold in contrast to the parching heat of the previous day. Carrying flashlights, we began our ascent of the mountain called Gebel Musa—"the mountain of Moses." As we slowly made our way, we recalled that *long ago* Moses left behind the children of Israel and came up these mountains to meet with God for the second time. After a two-hour climb, we arrived at the summit and waited quietly in the darkness for the transformation to take place. When the sun's rays finally illuminated the desert mountains, we viewed the spectacular scene that Moses would have seen centuries ago.

God's activity for and with Israel on Mount Sinai underlies all biblical religion. The covenant that God made with Israel there—called the Mosaic covenant or Sinai (Sinaitic) covenant—contains God's most comprehensive self-disclosure, revealing the meaning of His saving name, codifying His laws, and establishing forms of worship, including sacrifices, that would keep the covenant community in a covenant relationship with Him. The Sinai covenant is important both for Israel and for humanity as a whole.

An important question that emerges is whether the covenant at Mount

Sinai is totally new. Rather than describing it as new, we should consider it essentially a continuation, enlargement, and particularization of God's earlier covenants, containing essentially the same design, purpose, and goal for Israel's and humanity's redemption as the earlier covenants.

The Sinai (Mosaic) covenant was *not* a covenant of works. It was not intended to teach the ancient Israelites a way to achieve righteousness or justification by human merit or by human endeavor in keeping the law. Like the covenant that God made with Abraham and the other patriarchs, it, too, is a covenant of grace. It does indeed demand obedience; but the Abrahamic covenant also demanded obedience, as did the earlier Noachic covenant. But obedience in connection with the covenants that God has made is not a way to gain salvation but is, rather, a way of life to be lived by the redeemed through the enabling grace and power of God.

The obligations or conditions of the covenant God places on the members of His covenant community simply outline the community's way of life, once its members have experienced the redemption, salvation, and liberation by God. This way of life could be lived then, as today, only by the enabling grace and power of God. If we try to live this way solely by human endeavor, our efforts deteriorate into attempts to gain human merit—the kind of merit that God does not accept in His plan of redemption. Thus we may appreciate the following insight: "The covenant that God made with His people at Sinai is to be our refuge and defense. . . . This covenant is of just as much force today as it was when the Lord made it with ancient Israel."[1]

The God of the Sinai covenant

Exodus 19–24 contains not only the covenant that God made with the people of Israel after they left Egypt but also extraordinary insights into the nature of God.[2] It reveals that the God who is active in salvation is also a God who is in control of history. This biblical picture of God portrays Him as the Unseen Controller of all history and all circumstances. This God who manifests Himself in the opening chapters of

Exodus is a God in control of every circumstance of life—not merely of climactic points in the course of history but of every detail of individual lives. He overrules all events and shows Himself to be an invincible power over history. This overruling for the ultimate good of His children is part of God's saving activity and His loving providence manifested in the book of Exodus.

The stunning experience of the burning bush recorded in Exodus 3:1–12 contains the significant call of Moses to be God's instrument in negotiating the release of the Israelites from Egyptian slavery. Within this setting, Moses asked God what he should answer when Israel would ask, "What is his name?" (Exodus 3:13). We will discover the major importance of this question only after we understand the context and analyze the answer.

It should be noted that the word in the question translated "what" did not seek the title or designation of deity in terms of asking a mere name. If just a name is requested, the Hebrew uses the interrogative term *mî,* which if used in this passage would have simply inquired about God's literal name or title. But in the question Moses posed, the interrogative *māh* is used, and this type of interrogative seeks out the power, qualities, and character of God. "What Moses asks, then, has to do with whether God can accomplish what he is promising. What is there in his reputation that lends credibility to the claim in his call?"[3] The reader sensitive to the nuances of the Hebrew language will immediately understand that the answer sought by the question calls not for a name or a title or a designation but, rather, for the meaning of God's name: "I AM WHO I AM" (Exodus 3:14, RSV).

This pithy little sentence "I AM WHO I AM" is clearly a reference to the name Yahweh, but the clause puts new content into the word. It sets forth the meaning of God's name in a way never revealed before. The phrase expresses "being" but yet not as the ancient Greek philosophers expressed "pure being" in the philosophical sense—but, rather, "active being" in terms of revelation. This phrase also expresses the idea that God has been in the past and is in the present and will be in the future.

He is the God with whom the initiative always resides. We have already seen how God took the initiative in Creation and how He took the initiative once humankind fell into sin, moving in to reestablish communion with humanity. Now God again takes the initiative. He is the God independent of history and yet in control of history, independent of the future and yet in control of it.

Another central aspect of the nature and character of God was revealed to Moses as recorded in Exodus 6:28. In this passage, God says that prior to Moses' time, He had not made Himself known by the name of Yahweh. What does He mean? In the book of Genesis, God had repeatedly revealed Himself under the name Yahweh (Genesis 12:1, 7; 13:14; 15:2, 7), even stating explicitly to Abraham, "I am the LORD [Yahweh]" (Genesis 15:7). What does the statement to Moses mean?

In the entire experience leading up to and involving the Exodus and the aftermath, God attempted to reveal an aspect of His character additional to the one already expressed in earlier designations such as "Almighty God": "I appeared to Abraham, Isaac, and Jacob, as God Almighty, but by My name, LORD [Yahweh], I did not make Myself known to them" (Exodus 6:3, NASB). The intent of the statement is that God showed Himself to Abraham, Isaac, and Jacob in the character and significance of Almighty God, but in the character and significance of His name Yahweh, He had not previously made Himself known. The new aspect of God's character and its significance focused on here is that He will reveal Himself through redemption: in setting Israel free from bondage, in making them His special covenant people, and in providing the means for them to remain His covenant people through His grace and His enabling power.

Redemption and covenant

The great redemption event of the Exodus experience, God's act of freeing His people from Egyptian subjugation, is referred to as an act of His love. "Thou hast led in thy steadfast love the people whom thou hast redeemed" (Exodus 15:13, RSV). "Yea, he loved his people" (Deuteronomy

33:3, RSV). Israel was reminded that "the LORD loves you" (Deuteronomy 7:8, RSV). But God loves not only Israel or every member of those who belonged to Israel, He also loves the stranger or foreigner in her midst (Deuteronomy 10:18). God's love for His people, as expressed here, describes not an emotional or intellectual attitude but His saving and redeeming activity for humankind.

God, in His love, chooses or elects Israel. It is an act of God's gracious and loving initiative, just as in previous covenants made with the patriarchs. God's choice of Israel is not determined by any of Israel's characteristics or excellencies but, rather, it is based totally and grounded supremely in God giving His undeserved love and grace to His people Israel (Deuteronomy 4:37; 7:6–8). God's redemptive act rests solely in His nature and is a partial revelation of His character.

In the story of Israel's deliverance from Egypt, the experience of redemption precedes the making of the covenant. In other words, the relationship between covenant and redemption is unequivocal: Redemption precedes covenant-making. God told Moses to say to the people, "You have seen what I did to the Egyptians, and how I bore you on eagles' wings and brought you to myself" (Exodus 19:4, RSV). The point is that God had already redeemed Israel. He had liberated her from Egyptian bondage as an act of free grace and divine love. Love, election, and redemption are gifts of God totally undeserved by His people.

We do not want to leave the impression, however, that in the sequence of redemption followed by covenant, the two are separate and that covenant is not also an act of redemption. To the contrary, covenant making, the covenant that God made with Israel on Mount Sinai, is also an act of God's initiative in redemption. God first redeemed His people by liberating them from Egyptian slavery and bondage; then God engaged in another act of salvation and redemption by making a covenant with them. In every respect God's love, His initiative, His mercy, and His redemptive design, totally initiated and totally grounded in God Himself, come to the foreground.

Here one additional aspect needs brief consideration. Israel as a people had been supremely loved, sovereignly chosen, and miraculously redeemed. God did this in pursuance of and in fulfillment of the Abrahamic covenant (Exodus 2:24; 3:16; 6:4–8; Psalms 105:8–12, 42–45; 106:45). This correlation indicates that the Sinai covenant and the Abrahamic covenant do not sharply diverge from each other. The Abrahamic covenant cannot be designated as a covenant of grace and the Sinai covenant as a covenant of works. Both the Sinai and Abrahamic covenants are covenants of grace; both have the same spiritual relationship at its center: "I will take you for my people, and I will be your God; and you shall know that I am the LORD your God, who has brought you out from under the burdens of the Egyptians" (Exodus 6:7, RSV).

"If you will obey"

By the time Israel came to Mount Sinai, they had experienced God's miraculous interventions in their behalf time and again. They had been liberated from Egyptian bondage without having had to fight for their freedom. God was their Warrior: God had led them to the Red Sea and then through the sea on dry land. God had saved them from potential calamity. He had provided miraculous food for them in the wilderness (Exodus 16). He had prevented their sandals from wearing out while they walked over the rough desert stones (Deuteronomy 29:5). God had guided them step by step.

Now after having come to Mount Sinai, God made a proposal to Israel to make a covenant with them: "Now therefore, if you will obey my voice and keep my covenant, you shall be my own possession among all peoples" (Exodus 19:5, RSV). Israel had come this far through God's mighty acts in history, but now they had to decide the nature and direction of their own future. Would they attempt to "go it alone" from here on? Would the people of Israel decide now to make it in the world in their own strength? Would they decide to return to the "security" of Egypt, as some within their ranks actually suggested? Or would they pledge their allegiance to their saving God, Yahweh? Evidently, it was

64

one thing to be set free from slavery but quite another thing to remain free spiritually, physically, and otherwise. That great choice was God's proposal set before His people. Which way would they choose to go?

God designed that the covenant He offered to His people would establish the deepest, most profound, and most intimate relationship possible between Him as their God and them as His people. This sublime God-human relationship was to give to the people of Israel security, protection, and blessing in every sphere of life. The people of Israel were offered freedom in the fullest and most comprehensive sense—not to be subject to selfishness, to greed, to passion; not to be striving for moral and/or spiritual autonomy but to live a true life with God, a life filled with a most profound sense of belonging. But such comprehensive freedom demanded that they enter into a covenant relationship with God, a covenant of salvation and grace, only on the basis of which they could continue to function in a unique way, totally free and completely dedicated to their Lord.

Before we analyze Israel's response, we should consider briefly what the three aspects the Sinai covenant revealed about God's design, purpose, and plan for them: "If you obey me fully and keep my covenant, then out of all nations you will be my treasured possession. Although the whole earth is mine, you will be for me a kingdom of priests and a holy nation" (Exodus 19:5, 6, NIV).

First, God planned to make Israel a treasured possession, His "own possession" (RSV) or a "peculiar treasure" (KJV). These translations attempt to render into adequate English the single Hebrew term *s̆gullāh*, the word in the Old Testament used consistently to express the idea of Israel as a choice or treasured possession. In contrast to other types of possessions, namely, those that could not be moved, such as real estate, Israel became, through God's love and affection, His moveable treasure. Israel is God's own possession, personally gained and privately treasured. Israel is set aside for a marked purpose (Deuteronomy 7:6; 14:2; 26:18, 19). The idea of treasured possession thus implies special value and special relationship.

Second, and closely related to the first aspect, God wanted to make Israel a kingdom of priests. Although some interpreters suggest the translation "kingly priests" or "royal priests," the Hebrew expression literally translates "kingdom of priests." This expressed purpose seems to communicate that Israel was to function as a kingdom made up of priests. God's particular choice of one people, namely Israel, had behind it a purpose of universal proportions and import. Each Israelite, in one way or another, was to function as God's priestly agent to bring blessings to the nations of the entire world and to minister to their needs.

How tragic to compare this ideal with the way the story actually unfolded! Ancient Israel never fulfilled their divine destiny of becoming a "kingdom of priests." Later the apostle Peter applied the same descriptive phrase, "kingdom of priests" (1 Peter 2:9), to the New Testament church, and with the same implications. How does the story read today? Are we doing any better in fulfilling our task as God's chosen people to share heaven's saving message?

The third aspect expressed in God's covenant proposal to Israel was His design that they would become a "holy nation." Only once in the Old Testament is His purpose thus stated. Never again do we find in the Old Testament a reference to Israel as a "holy nation," though later in Deuteronomy, we find a number of instances of the modified expression "holy people" (Deuteronomy 7:6; 14:2, 21; 26:19; 28:9).

The fact that Israel was to be a holy nation instead of a secular nation rested on God's promise and design to make them holy by separating them from the remaining and surrounding nations. The Israel of the covenant was to be primarily a religious entity. The terminology of God's agreement with them emphasized that He would make them holy. This emphasis shows up particularly in Leviticus 19:2 and Ezekiel 36:25–28. Because God is holy, His people are likewise to be holy—that is, they are to live in a holy manner. In Deuteronomy 26:19 the Lord declared, "You [Israel] will be a people holy to the LORD your God, as he promised" (NIV). Obedience to God's commandments, included in the terms in the covenant, is revealed here as the result rather than the condition of being a "holy people." The Lord planned to establish Israel "as a people holy to himself" (Deuteronomy 28:9, RSV; compare 7:6–9) on the condition that they keep His commandments. But God makes commandment keeping and continual obedience possible by the promise of His covenant to make His people holy. He separated them from the world and separated them unto Himself and dwells in them by His Spirit. In this sense, holiness is not something to be achieved by human beings in their own strength and on the basis of their own endeavor but, rather, something received and reflected in the daily life of faith-obedience by those who have been called to be a holy people.

"We will do"

God had graciously given Israel an invitation to be His covenant people. He had offered them a covenant of grace. How would the people respond? "All the people answered together and said, 'All that the LORD has spoken we will do' " (Exodus 19:8, RSV; compare Exodus 24:3).

Israel solemnly promised the Lord to be obedient to Him and do everything that He had said. Was there anything wrong with their response, "We will do"? Was it not God's design for Israel to give a positive response to His offer? Yes, but our answer must be qualified by an additional observation about the response: its acceptability to the Lord depended also upon the people's unspoken intent and motivation. The motivation behind the response, "We will do," could make that response either legalistic and self-redeeming (which would reduce God's covenant to a covenant of works); or it could make the response nonlegalistic on the basis of Israel accepting God's intent and design for them. That is, in a nonlegalistic response, the Israelites would realize their total dependence on Him for mercy when they failed and for His assisting grace at all times for obedience.

The difference between these two possible motivations behind the response, "We will do," relates to (1) whether Israel would do what God had spoken out of her own strength and with the intent of obligating God to grant the covenant blessings as a merit earned by their own strength or (2) whether Israel would obey the covenant obligations by faith through the enabling grace mercifully provided by the Lord—and thus experience the covenant blessings as gracious gifts freely bestowed by God. The difference rests on the motivation of those who respond— whether ancient Israel or us today.

The apostle Paul made it abundantly clear in Romans 9:31, 32 that Israel pursued righteousness legalistically, attempting to achieve perfect fulfillment of the law in and by her own strength. This way of achieving righteousness caused Israel neither to arrive at the ideals and blessings prescribed by the law and promised in the covenant nor to gain the law-righteousness that they pursued. "God brought them to Sinai; He manifested His glory; He gave them His law, with the promise of great blessings on condition of obedience: [Exodus 19:5, 6 quoted]. The people did not realize the sinfulness of their own hearts, and that without Christ it was impossible for them to keep God's law; and they readily entered into covenant with God. Feeling that they were able to establish their own righteousness, they declared, 'All that the Lord hath said we will do, and be obedient.' Exodus 24:7."[4]

Ellen White perceptively and succinctly outlines with great certainty key elements to keep in mind about obedience through faith in Jesus Christ—the kind of righteousness acceptable in the sight of God and made possible through the covenant of grace: "Instead of going about to establish our own righteousness we accept the righteousness of Christ. His blood atones for our sins. His obedience is accepted for us. Then the heart renewed by the Holy Spirit will bring forth 'the fruits of the Spirit.' Through the grace of Christ we shall live in obedience to the law of God written upon our hearts. Having the Spirit of Christ, we shall walk even as He walked."[5]

The way of salvation for ancient Israel was the same as for the Christian today. The ancient Israelite was never in God's design and intent to be saved by his own obedience to the law. Nor can the Christian ever earn his or her salvation by obedience to the law. The purpose and design of obedience to the law is not to gain salvation. From its very origin, law is firmly set in the context of grace. The man or woman who has been saved by God will never want to live in disobedience to the law. But obedience is possible only through the assisting grace of God through Jesus Christ and the Holy Spirit. The relationship between covenant, grace, and law will be considered further in the next chapter.

---

1. Ellen G. White, "Comments," *Seventh-Day Adventist Bible Commentary*, vol. 1 (Hagerstown, MD: Review and Herald®, 1953), 1103.

2. On Israel's covenant with God at Sinai, see Michael G. Hasel, "Exodus," *Andrews Bible Commentary*, ed. Angel M. Rodríguez (Berrien Springs, MI: Andrews University Press, 2020), 217–225.

3. John I. Durham, *Exodus*, Word Biblical Commentary 3 (Waco, TX: Word Books, 1987), 38.

4. Ellen G. White, *Patriarchs and Prophets* (Mountain View, CA: Pacific Press®, 1958), 371, 372.

5. White, *Patriarchs and Prophets*, 372.

Eight

Covenant and Law
at Sinai

When we come to speak about covenant and law, we get into some of the most fundamental matters in faith and life. Over the centuries, some students of the Bible claim that God offered to Israel a covenant of works on Mount Sinai; that is, a covenant by which salvation or righteousness would be gained through human works and achievements. They contrast this covenant of works with the earlier covenant made with Abraham, where righteousness came by faith in God's achievements, but that faith was active in good works. If this theory is correct—if the Sinai covenant is indeed one of works—then why would Jesus have condemned the Jews for their legalism? Why would the Jews then be condemned if they simply followed that which the Lord had asked them to do?

Covenant contains law
For ancient Israel, as always in the Bible, God's saving, redeeming, and liberating activity preceded making the covenant and giving law or instruction.[1] We may state this truth another way: Law is God's specified way of life within the covenant between Himself and humankind. Thus God's covenant with its law—the two together—constitute God's

means of keeping His people in a state of redemption. They remain in this state, not by obeying the law through their own strength and discipline but, rather, by God's continuing presence, power, and activity of grace and mercy in their lives, enabling them to obey Him. Thus the divine covenant with its divine law provides the means of an ever-deepening and expanding experience of spiritual, mental, and physical well-being and growth for those who live and function within that covenantal relationship.

The self-identification on the part of God at the beginning of the Ten Commandments is, "I am the LORD your God, who brought you out of the land of Egypt, out of the house of slavery" (Exodus 20:2, NASB). This introduction to the Ten Commandments reveals the foundation for the relationship between God and His people. It places this relationship in the context of divine and unmerited redemption. So immediately before He gave the law on Mount Sinai, God called to remembrance the basis for law giving. It has been said that only this remembering can join gospel and law into one. The believer keeps the law because he or she remembers the salvation that God has already provided.

In God's design, the remembering is to result in a love response built upon faith that provides the motivation for obedience (Deuteronomy 6:5; Psalm 18:1; Jeremiah 2:2). The motivation for obedience is not to secure God's favor or to gain life in salvation. The law is not the agent to bring about salvation; and obedience has never been the means God designed for human beings to gain righteousness, salvation, and life. Obedience, or law, is an act of faith through which the believer confesses his love and loyalty to God. It is an act of faith through which the believer demonstrates that he or she is dependent upon the enabling power of God to obey, not only in external acts but also with the heart.

Covenant involves relationship and communion. No real relationship and no true communion can exist between two individuals without a set of norms defining the basis on which the relationship or communion is to be maintained. Likewise, a covenantal relationship between the redeeming God and His redeemed people can function only on the basis of established norms, obligations, or stipulations—in short, the law. The law defines the relationship and provides the terms for its successful continuance.

Law forms an integral part of the covenant. God gave specific instructions so that His people would understand what they were to do and not to do. "Say to the people of Israel, I am the LORD your God. You shall not do as they do in the land of Egypt, where you dwelt, and you shall not do as they do in the land of Canaan, to which I am bringing you. You shall not walk in their statutes. You shall do my ordinances and keep my statutes and walk in them. I am the LORD your God" (Leviticus 18:2–4, RSV). This passage makes the matter clear: The people in Egypt did what they did because they followed the gods of the Egyptians. The people in the land of Canaan acted in harmony with the gods they worshiped. But Israel, God's people, knew their God by the formula of self-presentation: "I am the LORD your God." Thus God instructed His people, "You shall not walk in their statutes. You shall do my ordinances and keep my statutes and walk in them."

The giving of the law is as much an act of grace as God's gift of election. The giving of the law is as much an act of mercy as the deliverance from Egyptian slavery. The gift of the law is as much an act of God's love as the making of the covenant to which the law belongs. The law thus becomes an instrument defining all relationships within the covenant and the covenant community. It defines the vertical God-man relationship. It also defines the horizontal human relationships. The law is God's divine instrument for defining relationships in which faith responds to love in obedience.

Throughout the Old Testament we find a most intimate interrelationship between covenant and law. When Moses addressed Israel, he noted that at Mount Sinai, the Lord "declared to you his covenant, which he commanded you to perform, that is, the ten commandments" (Deuteronomy 4:13, RSV). We see here an evident equation between covenant and Decalogue. In other instances, various words, such as *law* (Psalm 78:10; Isaiah 24:5; Hosea 8:1), *statutes* (Psalm 50:16; 2 Kings 17:15; Isaiah

24:5), *testimonies* (Psalms 25:10; 132:12), *commandments* (Psalm 103:18), and *word* in the sense of the Word of the Lord (Deuteronomy 33:9) are all found parallel or in closest association (if not in synonymous relationship) with the word *covenant* (*b^erît*). In Jeremiah, "the words of this covenant" (Jeremiah 11:3, 6, 8) are the words of God's law, statutes, testimonies, and commandments.

Law within the covenant

The Hebrew word for *law* (*Tôrāh*) appears in the Old Testament no less than 220 times. It must not be taken to mean "law" in the Latin sense of *lex*, meaning law of the empire. Nor is it to be understood as the Greeks understood their word for law (*nomos*), namely, that which had always been done. In the Hebrew language the term *Tôrāh* comes from the word *hôrâh*, meaning "to point out," "to teach," or "to instruct." Accordingly the noun *Tôrāh* means in its broadest sense "teaching" or "instruction." In this sense the word *law* signifies all the revealed will of God, or any part of it.

God gave Israel this instruction, this *Tôrāh*, in terms of "statutes and ordinances" (Deuteronomy 4:14, RSV) or "the testimonies, the statutes, and the ordinances" (verse 45, RSV) to regulate the life of Israel. *Tôrāh* is used in this sense frequently. Thus *law* could be a comprehensive kind of "instruction" that included all the laws: moral and ethical, civil and social, sacrificial and worship, and hygienic and health.

In other instances, *law (Tôrāh)*, can be used in a very narrow sense meaning only the Ten Commandments or Decalogue, also called "the words of the covenant" (Exodus 34:28). Containing the specifics and principles that are to govern both the God-man and human-human relationships, the Ten Commandments are all-inclusive and all-comprehensive for all spheres of life and experience.

Conditions of the covenant

In a number of explicit instances, we find in connection with the Sinai covenant certain "if" statements. "Now therefore, if you will obey my voice and keep my covenant, you shall be my own possession among all peoples" (Exodus 19:5, RSV). That little word "if" has extraordinary significance. It indicates that the Sinai covenant contained conditions. Opinions differ vastly on how these conditions are to be interpreted, but before we turn to this debate, it would be well to note a couple of additional statements that contain clear "if" statements. "If you walk in my statutes and observe my commandments and do them, then I will give you your rains. . . . But if you will not hearken to me, and will not do all these commandments . . . but break my covenant, I will do this to you: I will appoint over you sudden terror" (Leviticus 26:3, 4, 14–16, RSV).

Again in the book of Deuteronomy, we find another conditional promise: "You shall walk in all the way which the LORD your God has commanded you, that you may live, and that it may go well with you, and that you may live long in the land which you shall possess" (Deuteronomy 5:33, RSV).

The "if" statements are clearly conditional, involving obligations. But in giving the Sinai covenant, certainly obligatory in nature, God did not break new ground for establishing a relationship between Himself and His people. It was not a covenant of works in which man could now earn his salvation and life by obedience to the will of God. It was not a covenant built upon human merit, which would obligate God to fulfill His promises. The conditional aspect of the Sinai covenant is identical with the intent of the conditional statements of the Abrahamic covenant (see Genesis 17:9, 14; 18:19; 22:16–18; 26:4, 5), which is clearly a "covenant of grace."

These passages in connection with Abraham and the Abrahamic covenant make it abundantly clear that Abraham and his descendants were to live in a covenantal relationship with God in which man was justified by faith (Genesis 15:6). This faith relationship manifested itself or resulted in obedience caused by faith and made possible through God's grace. Genuine faith produces obedience: "Abraham obeyed my voice, and kept my charge, my commandments, my statutes, and my laws"

(Genesis 26:5). We must understand that "the covenant with Abraham also maintained the authority of God's law."[2] Thus the Abrahamic covenant is also conditional. The covenant is not unilateral in the sense that the fulfillment of the promises depended solely upon God, irrespective of the human partner's actions.

Unfortunately, the "if" statements in Exodus 19:5; Leviticus 26:3–45; Deuteronomy 11:13–17; and 28:1–68 can easily be misinterpreted and misunderstood in a legalistic way. One could understand the passages to imply that physical and eternal life and God's blessing are automatically guaranteed upon obedience, regardless of the inner disposition of the heart. However, the intent of the "if" statements is not a cold, mechanical legalism but a true covenant relationship with God involving right motives in both heart and mind.

Israel was to "keep the commandments of the LORD your God, by walking in his ways and by fearing him" (Deuteronomy 8:6, RSV). It was out of a sense and experience of gratitude to the Lord that Israel was to "love" Him (Deuteronomy 6:5; 10:12; 11:1, 13, 22; 13:3; etc.) and to "cleave" to Him (Deuteronomy 10:20; 11:22; 13:4; etc.). Blessing was to follow in the wake of obedience. Although blessing was conditional upon obedience, it could not be earned by a legalistic keeping of the law.

Obedience, life, and blessing

One of the most difficult passages for some students to harmonize with the scriptural teaching of salvation by grace is Leviticus 18:5, "So you shall keep My statutes and My judgments, by which a man may live if he does them; I am the LORD" (NASB). In essence, only two ways exist by which humans may gain or attempt to gain salvation. One way is salvation by works—righteousness gained by keeping the law. And the other is salvation by faith—righteousness received by faith through God's grace.

When one receives life (according to Leviticus 8:1–5) or blessing (according to Deuteronomy 28:1, 2), is this due to an act of human merit in which obedience to the law earns the blessing? Or is the blessing that overtakes the doer of the law a gift of God's grace?

It may help to go to Paul's use of Leviticus 18:5 in Romans 10:5. It appears that in his series of quotations in Romans 10:6–8, as well as in Romans 10:5, the apostle Paul is waging warfare against the lifestyle maintained by the Pharisees. A careful study of Romans 10:6–8 seems to indicate that Deuteronomy 30:11–14, which he quotes, should not be misinterpreted in the pharisaical manner, namely, that human beings are saved by works of law. It seems to be evident that the apostle Paul also is affirming in the previous verse, Romans 10:5, that Leviticus 18:5 should be understood in a way that differed radically from the interpretation held by mainstream Judaism.

Paul seems to suggest that the requirement to do righteousness is not fulfilled by such superhuman achievements as "to climb into heaven" or "to climb down into the abyss," which was Paul's way of describing the Jews' impossible attempts to produce and fulfill the righteousness of the law by their own efforts and merits. Paul then continues to suggest that the righteousness required by the law is fulfilled through the word, which is in the heart and in the mouth—which, according to Romans 10:10, is faith and confessing the Lord: "For with the heart one believes [and this leads] to righteousness, and with a mouth one confesses [and this leads] to salvation" (author's translation).

The life that Moses promises in Leviticus 18:5 seems, according to Romans 10:5–10, to be enjoyed by those who believe and confess. The obedience of faith thus becomes the proper fulfilling of the law, which requires righteousness and promises life to those who do righteousness. If our understanding of Paul's emphasis on Leviticus 18:5 and his interpretation of it in Romans 10:5–10 is correct—that the obedience of the law that results in the enjoyment of life promised in Leviticus 18:5 is the obedience of faith—then we have the biblical and divinely intended meaning of this particular text. In other words, the Jewish, pharisaic way of understanding this text as implying that keeping the law brought man into a right relationship with God is entirely mistaken. Paul argued correctly that the keeping of the law is the fruit of a right relationship with God rather than the means to earn or merit a right relationship with God. Paul's exegesis of Leviticus 18:5 is faithful to that text's original setting. The law was given to the covenant people after their redemption from Egypt (Leviticus 18:3), not as a moral hurdle to be cleared or a meritorious activity to be performed if they wished to be saved but as a description of the love-motivated lifestyle of God's redeemed people.

Paul showed that "righteousness by law" in the sense of the human perversion to establish righteousness by legalistic obedience is not what the Old Testament taught at all. Paul is contrasting the divine way of "righteousness by faith" with the human attempt at "righteousness by law," which is a legalistic misuse, misunderstanding, and misinterpretation of the law along Jewish and pharisaical lines. Paul shows that the righteousness set forth by the law, which is "holy, and just, and good" (Romans 7:12), was righteousness by faith, or obedience by faith. "Many commentators have found difficulty in the fact that Paul uses words of Moses which seem to pertain only to the law, to describe righteousness by faith. . . . The problem is resolved by recognizing that righteousness by faith has always been God's method for saving man and that the giving of the law through Moses was an integral part of this plan. . . . Consequently, it is quite unreasonable to assume that Moses was ignorant of the proper relationship between the law and the gospel and that whenever he spoke so strongly of obedience to God's commandments he was commending righteousness by law rather than by faith."[3]

Paul effectively exposes the legalistic and pharisaic perversion of the law by those who depend upon their own fulfillment of the law for justification before God. He uses the words of Moses himself from Leviticus 18:5 to remind the legalists that while righteousness comes by faith, it is a faith that issues or manifests itself in obedience. But such obedience believers are not able to render unaided, without the enabling grace provided by God through the Holy Spirit. In short, the problem with Leviticus 18:5 is not that it teaches that the enjoyment of life is dependent upon self-merited obedience. A legalistic interpretation has imposed this meaning on the text, which the text itself does not intend.

The obedience to the law that results in the enjoyment of life as promised in Leviticus 18:5 is the obedience of faith. It is not legalism or salvation by works; but, rather, it is salvation by faith from which issues obedience. Thus it is evident that the way of salvation in the Old Testament and the way of salvation in the New Testament are the same—both being salvation by grace through faith, which results in obedience.

---

1. On the law, see Mario Veloso, "The Law of God," *Handbook of Seventh-day Adventist Theology*, Commentary Reference Series, vol. 12, ed. Raoul Dederan (Hagerstown, MD: Review and Herald®, 2000), 457–492.

2. Ellen G. White, *Patriarchs and Prophets* (Mountain View, CA: Pacific Press®, 1958), 370.

3. F. D. Nichols, ed., *Seventh-day Adventist Bible Commentary*, vol. 6 (Washington, DC: Review and Herald®, 1956), 597.

Nine

The Sabbath—
Sign and Seal of God

The search for the origin of the Sabbath outside of Scripture has been disappointing. The search began during the nineteenth century, when archaeological discoveries of Babylonian texts prompted the search for Sabbath origins in that geographical location and time. Others searched for its origins in Ugaritic texts from Syria, from the Midianites in Sinai, and elsewhere. The consensus about the search for the origin of the Sabbath is that there is no consensus.[1] It appears to be unique as a biblical institution originating at Creation and reaffirmed at Sinai.

The seventh-day Sabbath functions as a sign of the covenant that God made with His people (Exodus 13:17). Sabbath celebration provides a special palace in time for communication and communion with God, and in its wake, it brings physical, mental, and spiritual regeneration.[2] It also provides freedom and liberation from work, from competition, and from the tensions of everyday existence. In summary, it brings rest and renewal.

Those who keep the Sabbath acknowledge God as their covenant Lord—the Lord of their lives. They acknowledge God as their Redeemer and Sanctifier. Through that acknowledgment, they give up any claim that Sabbath keeping is a way to gain life. Yet their obedience indicates that keeping the law by the enabling power of God is the proper way of life for each true son and daughter of God.

The Sabbath is a covenant sign with three time dimensions. It carries significance for the here and now; it reflects on the past; and it reaches into the future. It reflects back in that it was instituted at Creation and is a memorial of God's creation of this world. It says something significant relating to God's activity in the present, confirming as a covenant sign in the lives of those who acknowledge God as their Lord that they have accepted His Lordship and redemption and that they live as they do by His power. Then the Sabbath reaches into the ultimate future, finding its complete fulfillment in the plan of salvation, when total, unlimited freedom and final redemption will be experienced.

The marvelous redeeming and sanctifying qualities inherent in the Sabbath direct us from God's "very good" (Genesis 1:31) creation in the beginning to a most glorious future of unhindered communion and unlimited access with both the Father and the Lord Jesus Christ. The Sabbath links Creation (Genesis 2:2, 3) with new creation (Isaiah 66:23). As such a link, it points forward to the future as a guarantee of a new heaven and a new earth, where the redeemed will enjoy uninterrupted, face-to-face fellowship with God forever and ever.

The origin of the Sabbath

We read in both Testaments that the seventh-day Sabbath has its origin at the Creation of the world. This truth is affirmed in the Old Testament in Genesis 2:2, 3: "By the seventh day God completed His work which He had done; and He rested on the seventh day from all His work which He had done. Then God blessed the seventh day and sanctified it, because in it He rested from all His work which God had created and made" (NASB). The New Testament reaffirms in the words of Jesus and the apostles the fact that the seventh-day Sabbath has its origin in Eden (Mark 2:27; Hebrews 4:1–11).

Both Sabbath keepers and non-Sabbath keepers have long recognized that the seventh day mentioned in Genesis 2:2, 3 is the seventh-day

Sabbath. Note a contemporary example: "The word 'sabbath' is not employed [in Genesis 2:2, 3]; but it is certain that the author [of Genesis] meant to assert that God blessed and hallowed the seventh day as the Sabbath."[3]

God "rested" on the Sabbath. Was God in need of physical rest? Was God worn out after His work of creation during Creation week? What was God's real purpose in resting on the seventh day of Creation week? It would be ludicrous to suggest that God had become tired, because God never tires, according to the Bible. Thus God's purpose for resting on the Sabbath could not have been that He needed physical rest.

It would be biblical to suggest that God rested on the seventh day to provide a divine example for human beings to follow. We must keep in mind that the seventh day of Creation week was the first full day of Adam and Eve's lives. God took time on their first full day of life to engage in fellowship and communion with them by providing a day of rest, a routine that was to be followed on each seventh day of a seven-day cycle from then on.

The pattern that God established for human beings by being our Example in rest indicates that we also are to work for six days and then rest on the seventh-day Sabbath. The Sabbath becomes a weekly high point, designed to call us aside from our regular activities of providing livelihood, protection, and care for ourselves and for our fellow human beings, to communicate in a special way with the Creator, who also is our Savior.

Another important idea expressed in Genesis 2:2, 3 is that God "sanctified" or "hallowed" or "made holy" the seventh day. What does the idea of making the seventh-day Sabbath holy communicate? Is it to provide this day with a magical quality of holiness, present only on this particular day? The basic meaning of "making holy" or "sanctifying" suggests that the term, as used here, describes an act of God in setting this day apart from all other days for the purpose of the sanctifying presence of the Creator.

The holiness with which the Sabbath is imbued connotes a special manifestation of God's presence on this particular day. The Sabbath holiness and God's holiness and the holiness of God's people are all in one way or another interrelated. God's purpose for asking His people to "observe my Sabbaths" is because "I am the LORD, who makes you holy" (Exodus 31:13, NIV). God's holiness, man's holiness, and the holiness of the Sabbath all belong together.

It is also stated that God "blessed" the Sabbath. The idea of blessing in Scripture is extremely rich. In the Old Testament, the word for *blessing* generally denotes a bestowal of some material good (Deuteronomy 11:26; 28:1–14; Proverbs 10:22; 28:20). But it also is sed in other situations. For example, we find such expressions as "blessed be . . . my people" (Isaiah 19:25). Only rarely do we find that the Old Testament God blesses things: Once, it was recorded that the Lord blessed the fields (Genesis 27:27) and, once, that He blessed the animals (Genesis 1:22).

Only in Genesis 2:3 and in Exodus 20:11, is it stated that God blessed the Sabbath. Probably this means that through the Sabbath, the Lord mediates the divine blessing to the person who keeps the Sabbath day and who thus joins himself to the Lord in a covenant relationship. This implication would seem to assure anyone who enters into fellowship and communion with God by keeping His Sabbath that he or she will be blessed with fullness of life in the physical, mental, and spiritual spheres.

Sabbath and manna

It is interesting that the familiar story of God giving manna to Israel, as reported in Exodus 16, is the setting in which God teaches the Israelites before Sinai the importance of Sabbath keeping. The incidental manner in which the Sabbath is introduced in Exodus 16 and the emphasis that the Lord places upon it for proving "whether they will walk in my law or not" (Exodus 16:4, RSV) implies that the Sabbath was previously known. This is the point made by G. H. Waterman: "In fact, the equation of the sabbath with the seventh day, the statement that the Lord gave the Israelites the sabbath, and the record that the people, at God's command, rested on the seventh day all point unmistakably to the primeval institution of the sabbath."[4]

God chooses the miraculous gift of the manna (Exodus 16:4–30) as the occasion to teach the greater, perpetual gift of the Sabbath. In at least three ways, the gift of the manna served to identify the Sabbath and emphasize its holy character: First, a regular portion of manna fell each day; but on the sixth day, a double portion was provided. Second, no manna fell on the Sabbath day. Third, the portion kept over from the sixth day for the Sabbath was preserved unspoiled, while any kept over from other days would spoil.

Sabbath and commandment

In a real sense, the Ten Commandments constitute the heart of the five books of Moses, if not of the entire Scripture.[5] They provide God's foundation for life, defining man's relationship with his fellowmen and with God. The larger setting for giving the Ten Commandments in Exodus 20 is God making a covenant with His people. In this sense, the Decalogue provides a legal basis for the covenant relationship. But this interrelation must be understood in its true role.

It may be advantageous to understand the legal aspect of the covenant relationship in a sense similar to that of the wedding license in a contract of marriage. A marriage may be legalized by a wedding license; but it becomes a true marital relationship only when the legal terms of the contract are fleshed out with love as the partners share life together. So the Decalogue as law is legally binding, though not in a restrictive sense. Its terms represent God's love for human beings and represent God's nature and character.

The Ten Commandments called, in turn, for a response of love from Israel (see Deuteronomy 6:4, 5). It has been stated with deep insight that the Ten Commandments were "representative of God's love in that its injunctions, both negative and positive, led not to restriction of life, but to fullness of life. It demanded a response of love, not because obedience would somehow accumulate credit in the sight of God, but because the grace of God, experienced already in the liberation from Egypt and in the divine initiative in the covenant promise, elicited such a response from man in gratitude."[6]

We will now focus our attention on the fourth commandment: "Remember the sabbath day, to keep it holy. Six days you shall labor and do all your work, but the seventh day is a sabbath of the LORD your God; in it you shall not do any work, you or your son or your daughter, or your male servant or your female servant or your cattle or your sojourner who stays with you. For in six days the LORD made the heavens and the earth, the sea and all that is in them, and rested on the seventh day; therefore the LORD blessed the sabbath day and made it holy" (Exodus 20:8–11, NASB).

This commandment is the longest of the ten and stands at the center of the Decalogue. In it, God gives a positive command: "Six days you shall labor and do all your work" (verse 9). This positive command finds its analogue in the "shall not" command of verse 10, where the Lord states clearly: "You shall not do any work, you or your son or your daughter, your male servant or your female servant or your cattle or your sojourner who stays with you." Thus we have two commands here: one stating that people are to labor six days and the other that they shall not labor or do any work on the seventh day. Similarly, we have in this commandment two motivations for keeping the Sabbath, each complementing and amplifying the other. The first one, positive also in its slant, indicates that God would want man to do all his labor in the first six days of the week *because the seventh day is the Sabbath to the Lord.* The second motivation begins with a negative prohibition but ends positively by linking the prohibition from doing any work on the Sabbath day to the fact that the Lord Himself created everything in six days and rested on the seventh day Himself.

In the wording of the Sabbath commandment as reiterated by Moses in Deuteronomy 5:12–15, we also note two motivations. The first, stated in verse 14, is identical to the first motivation in the Exodus 20 wording: "The seventh day is a sabbath of the LORD your God" (NASB).

But the second is significantly different, as given in verse 15: "You shall remember that you were a slave in the land of Egypt, and the LORD your God brought you out of there by a mighty hand and by an outstretched arm" (NASB).

The difference should be recognized for what it is and should not be overemphasized. The Exodus reference is to God's creative work undertaken in six days during Creation week. To rest on the Sabbath was to remember that human beings, as part of God's created order, were totally dependent on the Creator. The creation theme, as various scholars have emphasized, is also present in the Deuteronomy 5 account. In this passage, reference is made to the Exodus from Egypt that marks in effect "the creation of God's people as a nation, and the memory of that event was also a reminder to the Israelites of their total dependence upon God."[7]

Thus Exodus 20 refers to the Creation at the beginning of the world; and Deuteronomy 5 refers to another beginning, the beginning of God's people. In other words, a profound thematic relationship exists between the motivation in Exodus 20 and in Deuteronomy 5 as regards the Sabbath. Creation is the common theme—God's creative power.

Sabbath—a covenant sign

The creation theme appears not only in Exodus 20:11 and in Deuteronomy 5:15 but it also recurs in Exodus 31:16, 17 in connection with the Sabbath as a sign between the Lord and His people, a covenant sign: "The Israelites are to observe the Sabbath, celebrating it for the generations to come as a lasting covenant. It will be a sign between me and the Israelites forever, for in six days the LORD made the heavens and the earth, and on the seventh day he abstained from work and rested" (Exodus 31:16, 17, NIV). In the Old Testament, the Sabbath is designated four times as a "sign" (see Exodus 31:13, 17; Ezekiel 20:12, 20).

What does it mean for the Sabbath to be a "sign"? In English *sign* can have several meanings. In its broadest scope, it applies to an action, condition, quality occurrence, or visible object that points to a fact or conveys a meaning. It is appropriate to understand the Sabbath as a sign in the sense in which the Scripture uses the term *sign*. To determine this sense, we will investigate a few of the seventy-eight times in the Old Testament in which the term is used.

In three instances, we have signs associated with covenants. The first such sign is the rainbow (Genesis 9:12, 13, 17). Then we find "sign" connected with circumcision in the covenant made with Abraham (Genesis 17:11). And the third instance associates "sign" with "covenant" in reference to the Sabbath as a sign of the covenant that God made with His people on Mount Sinai in Exodus 31 (see also Ezekiel 20). By assigning to these events in the history of salvation certain characteristics or by assigning to these events the character of a sign, these events and the phenomena associated with them take on value far beyond the subject and the event themselves.

The Sabbath is a covenant sign "between me and you throughout your generations" (Exodus 31:13; compare Ezekiel 20:12), the Lord had said to Israel. The person who keeps the Sabbath in the right spirit thereby signifies that he or she stands in a saved relationship with God.

The Sabbath as a sign imparts to the believer first of all the knowledge that the Lord is his covenant God. It also indicates that the Lord "sanctifies" His people (Leviticus 20:8; 21:8; 22:32; Ezekiel 37:28) by making them His "holy" people (Exodus 19:6; Deuteronomy 7:6; Leviticus 19:2, 3).

The Sabbath as a sign of divine sanctification needs further amplification. Let us look more closely at Exodus 31:13, a Sabbath text that explicitly states, "You shall keep my sabbaths, for this is a sign between me and you throughout your generations, that you may know that I, the LORD, sanctify you" (RSV). An entirely new aspect of the Sabbath as a sign is emphasized here, the idea of the Sabbath as a "sign" of sanctification. A person who looks at Sabbath keeping in a legalistic or pharisaic way may think that the Sabbath keeping itself will sanctify him or her. Not at all. The Lord does the sanctifying, the text says. That sanctification is an act on the part of the Lord *for* His people must never be overlooked.

The sanctification process is as much the work of God's redemptive love as is Heaven's saving and redemptive work through Christ. Righteousness and sanctification are both activities of God. "I, the LORD, sanctify you." Thus the Sabbath is a sign that imparts the knowledge of God as Sanctifier. "The Sabbath given to the world as the sign of God as the Creator is also the sign of Him as the Sanctifier."[8]

The second new idea in Exodus 31:13 is that the Sabbath is a sign of knowledge: "That you may know." The Hebrew concept of knowledge is extremely broad. Knowledge contains intellectual, relational, and emotional aspects. "To know" does not simply mean to know a fact intellectually, particularly when a person is the object. It means to have a meaningful relationship with the one known. Thus "to know the Lord" means to be consciously in the right relationship with Him. It means to "serve" Him (1 Chronicles 28:9); it means to "fear" Him (Isaiah 11:3; Psalm 119:79; Proverbs 1:7); it means to "believe" Him (Isaiah 43:10); it means to "trust" Him (Psalm 9:10); it means to "seek" Him (Psalm 9:10); and it means to "call on" His name (Jeremiah 10:25; Psalm 79:6).

The text states clearly that the Sabbath is a sign of the covenant between God and His people throughout all of their generations for the purpose that "you may know that I, the LORD, sanctify you" (Exodus 31:13, RSV). The Sabbath as a sign in respect to knowledge relates to the fact that the Lord is known as the One who sanctifies His people. It is God who makes His people holy. This knowledge is saving knowledge. The believer who truly understands the meaning of the Sabbath and Sabbath keeping understands that the Lord of the Sabbath is also his Lord. His Lord is the Creator. His Lord is the Redeemer. His Lord is also the Sanctifier.

The Sabbath functions in yet another sense as a sign. It serves as a mark of separation, indicating to people of other religions or to people who do not keep the Sabbath that a unique relationship exists between God and His Sabbath-keeping people. Functioning as a sign of recognition, the Sabbath separates His people from the rest of humankind unto God. As Cain was recognized by the sign that God put on him, so God's people are recognized by the Sabbath that keeps them separated unto God for service to the world.

The pen of Ellen White has aptly captured a major aspect of this particular function of the Sabbath as a sign: "By keeping His Sabbath holy we are to show that we are His people. His Word declares the Sabbath to be a sign by which to distinguish the commandment-keeping people. . . . Those who keep the law of God will be one with Him in the great controversy commenced in heaven between Satan and God."[9] The Sabbath is a sign of separation and a distinguishing mark of God's people, making them visible within the sphere of the great controversy between the powers of good and the powers of evil.

Sabbath—seal of God

It has been recognized, time and again, that the Sabbath commandment is found at the center of the Ten Commandments. How appropriate, since it relates to both the divine-human dimension and the human-human dimension! It is also appropriate as analogous with the position of seals on ancient official documents. The Sabbath commandment identifies the Lord of the Sabbath in a special way and indicates His sphere of authority and ownership. In these two aspects—namely, (1) the identity of Deity as Yahweh (LORD), who is the Creator (Exodus 20:11; 31:17) and who thus holds a unique place and (2) the sphere of His ownership and authority over "heaven and earth, the sea, and all that is in them" (Exodus 20:11, RSV; compare 31:17)—the Sabbath commandment has the characteristics of a typical seal on international, ancient Near Eastern treaty documents. These seals are typically in the center or middle of the treaty documents and also contain (1) the identity of the deity in whose name the treaty is sworn (usually a pagan god) and (2) the sphere of ownership and authority (usually a limited geographical area).

By analogy, the Sabbath functions as a "sign" (Exodus 31:13, 17) or, in this instance rather, as a seal between God and His people ("between me and you") and is thus the seal of the relationship between God and His own people. This is significant for the believer because in keeping the seventh-day Sabbath, as did our Lord at the end of Creation week, the believer acknowledges Him as Creator and Re-creator (Redeemer and Sanctifier). The believer also acknowledges God's ownership and authority over all creation, even over himself. It makes the believer part of God's covenant community of true worshipers.

These are but a few of the highlights of the riches of the Sabbath within the covenant.[10] The Sabbath is truly a gift from God for human beings. It provides divinely appointed time for human rest within the restlessness of humankind.

---

1. See the detailed discussions about Sabbath origins in Gerhard F. Hasel, "The Sabbath in the Pentateuch," *The Sabbath in Scripture and History*, ed. Kenneth A. Strand (Washington, DC: Review and Herald®, 1982), 21–43; Hasel, "Sabbath," *Anchor Bible Dictionary*, vol. 5, ed., D. N. Freedman (New York: Doubleday, 1992), 849–856; Hasel, "The Origin of the Biblical Sabbath and the Historical-Critical Method: A Methodological Case Study," *Journal of the Adventist Theological Society* 4/1 (1993): 17–46.

2. See the development of this concept in Abraham Joshua Heschel, *The Sabbath: Its Meaning for Modern Man* (New York: Noonday Press, 1951), 13–24.

3. G. H. Waterman, "Sabbath," *Zondervan Pictorial Encyclopedia of the Bible*, vol. 5, ed., Merrill C. Tenney (Grand Rapids, MI: Zondervan, 1975), 183.

4. Waterman, "Sabbath," 184.

5. On the Ten Commandments, see Michael G. Hasel, "Exodus," *Andrews Bible Commentary*, ed. Angel M. Rodríguez (Berrien Springs, MI: Andrews University Press, 2020), 218–221.

6. P. C. Craigie, *The Book of Deuteronomy* (Grand Rapids, MI: Eerdmans, 1976), 150.

7. Craigie, *The Book of Deuteronomy*, 157.

8. Ellen G. White, *Testimonies for the Church*, vol. 6 (Mountain View, CA: Pacific Press®, 1948), 350.

9. Ellen G. White, *Selected Messages*, book 2 (Hagerstown, MD: Review and Herald®, 2006), 160.

10. On the importance of the Sabbath amidst challenges today, see Frank M. Hasel and Michael G. Hasel, *How to Interpret Scripture* (Nampa, ID: Pacific Press, 2019), 73–81.

Ten

The
New Covenant

The new covenant is of pivotal significance for the believer because its focus is on Jesus Christ. It has been said repeatedly that a new covenant implies an old covenant. This raises the question of the newness of the new covenant. The expressions "new covenant" and "old covenant" imply both an aspect of continuity and an aspect of discontinuity. Continuity between the new and the old covenants is certainly implied in the phraseology itself—by the word *covenant* in both. The various points about discontinuity between the "new covenant" and "old covenant" seem primarily to rest on the adjectives *new* and *old*.[1]

In our investigation of the "new covenant" in this chapter, we will attempt to examine the differences between the respective covenants. In similar investigations, some theologians and Bible students have used the term "covenant of works" to designate the "old covenant." Correspondingly, they designate the "new covenant" using the term "covenant of grace." The "new covenant" is virtually equated with the "covenant of grace."

The two words *grace* and *works* indicate for many interpreters the radical distinction between two ways of salvation. Supposedly, one way whereby we are saved is through meritorious works; the other way is through the grace of God bestowed in Jesus Christ. Those who make a distinction between the "covenant of grace" and the "covenant of works" usually refer the latter to the period that began at Mount Sinai and assume God designed Israel to be saved by their works. In other words, their viewpoint is that Israel was saved by works and obedience. The "covenant of grace," in their viewpoint, designates salvation by grace, a salvation in which works have no meritorious, saving quality.

Announcement of the new covenant

It may surprise even careful Bible students to learn that the designation "new covenant" appears only once in the Old Testament. The great prophet Jeremiah, who prophesied during the last days of the kingdom of Judah when the people of God were about to go into Babylonian captivity, announced through the word of the Lord that a new covenant would come: "Behold, the days are coming, says the LORD, when I will make a new covenant with the house of Israel and the house of Judah, not like the covenant which I made with their fathers when I took them by the hand to bring them out of the land of Egypt, my covenant which they broke, though I was their husband, says the LORD" (Jeremiah 31:31, 32, RSV).

Even though the covenant is described with the adjective *new* for the first time in Jeremiah 31:31 (the one time in all the Old Testament), earlier prophets had already spoken about the new covenant. About 150 years before Jeremiah was sent by God to be His messenger to the southern kingdom of Judah, the prophet Hosea in the northern kingdom of Israel predicted a new covenant also: "In that day I will also make a covenant for them with the beasts of the fields, the birds of the sky, and the creeping things of the ground. And I will abolish the bow, the sword, and war from the land, and will make them lie down in safety. And I will betroth you to Me forever; yes, I will betroth you to Me in righteousness and in justice, in lovingkindness and in compassion, and I will betroth you to Me in faithfulness. Then you will know the LORD" (Hosea 2:18–20, NASB).

The phrase "in that day" introduced the prophet's prediction. It is a formula or an expression that points to the future. The prediction does not indicate when this future day would come but does communicate that such a day is decisively fixed in God's plan. "In that day" denotes the end of an old order of things and the beginning of the new age with a new order of things. The picture in Hosea 2:18 of a future covenant involving the animal kingdom as well as people and promising abolition of weapons of war and the introduction of peace, is certainly a picture of the future Messianic reign of peace.

Mention of the new covenant also brings to mind the rich statements found in various parts of the Old Testament about the new heart. For example, the Lord will provide "a heart to know that I am the LORD" (Jeremiah 24:7, RSV) and "one heart and one way" (Jeremiah 32:39, RSV). Also God will "take the stony heart out of their flesh and give them a heart of flesh" (Ezekiel 11:19, RSV) and will give "a new heart" and "a new spirit" (Ezekiel 36:26, RSV).

These statements remind us of the change that will take place in the lives of human beings when the new covenant comes into effect. So the Lord says, "I will put My Spirit within you" (Ezekiel 36:27, NASB). This work of God within humankind, within the hearts of men and women, provides the foundation for the activity, receptiveness, and significance of the "new covenant" in human lives. Hosea and Isaiah, the great prophets in the eighth century BC along with the great prophets who followed them later, namely, Jeremiah and Ezekiel, prophesy each in his own way about the new-covenant experience, though only one actually uses the designation *new*.

New covenant partners

Comparison of the "old covenant," which God made with ancient Israel on Mount Sinai, with the "new covenant" indicates several lines of continuity. The God is the same in both. He who makes the "new covenant" is the same covenanting God who had made the earlier covenant. In the prophecy of Jeremiah 31:31–34, the Lord of the Exodus clearly

The New Covenant

introduces Himself as again acting in covenant making when He explicitly states, "I will make a new covenant" (verse 31). Thus we see that the initiative of the new covenant is taken again by God, the same covenant-making God who has shown Himself previously.

It is always the saving God who initiates that which is new and seeks to bring salvation to those who distort His plan or reject His great gift. It is clear, once again, that the covenant that God makes with His people; that is, the new covenant, is a covenant that He initiates and that He makes. It is for this reason that we can speak of the biblical God as the covenant-making God. We can also speak of the biblical God as the Initiator of salvation in covenant making.

And the promise of divine fellowship and communion in the new covenant is the same as in the prior covenant that God made with Israel (compare Exodus 19:5, RSV, "You shall be my own possession"). The words "I will be their God," so typical of the God who had made the covenant with Israel at Sinai, find expression again in the "new covenant" passage in Jeremiah 31:33: "I will be their God, and they shall be my people" (RSV).

The partners are the same in both covenants—God, on the one hand, and His people, on the other. The new covenant is announced by the prophet as being made "with the house of Israel, and with the house of Judah" or simply with "the house of Israel" (see Jeremiah 31:31, 33). Although some take this to mean that the "new covenant" is only for the ancient nation of Israel, such is not the case. True, the Lord offered the "new covenant" first to His people whom He had elected and with whom He had made a covenant on Mount Sinai in the time of Moses. The Israelites, tragically, had turned that Sinai covenant into a law method of salvation, or justification by works. They endeavored to be righteous through their own futile strivings, not availing themselves of the method of faith that issues unto obedience. (In faith-obedience, the works and good deeds of the obedient person do not merit salvation but are the result of a salvation granted and given by God.) So God eventually had to turn from ethnic Israel to spiritual Israel to find the cooperation He

93

needed in putting into operation the provisions and benefits of His everlasting covenant, now called the new covenant.

The human partners in God's new covenant are now those who have the law of God written within their hearts, regardless of their ethnic background. "I will write it upon their hearts," God promises (Jeremiah 31:33, RSV). This internalizing of the "law"—the same law that God had proclaimed on Mount Sinai and had used in making the new covenant with ethnic Israel at that time—is nothing else but the internalizing of God's will and character.

The internalizing of God's law within the believer does not mean that God forces His will upon His people. The fact that God will write the law inwardly, making it a part of the total person and his or her will, demonstrates the principle of choice on the person's part. God will not now, and has never in the past, force His law into anyone's heart. The choice to have God's law written upon one's heart is an individual choice, made solely by each person. It is crucial, however, that the human partners with whom the new covenant is made and who will experience and stand within the new-covenant relationship understand this choice.

The members of the new-covenant community are not every physical or blood descendant of Abraham but every person who allows God to write His law inwardly, making it part of the total will of the believer so that he or she may obey God by faith. Thus the choice of allowing the law to be written upon the heart identifies that person as a member of God's spiritual Israel, where physical lineage is irrelevant. Any person who allows God to do His work within him or her becomes a member of God's Israel, His true, spiritual Israel. The true, spiritual Israel who have experienced God writing His law upon their hearts become partners with God in the new covenant.

In the New Testament those Jews who received Jesus Christ and His gospel for a time made up the kernel of the church (see Matthew 18:17). Thus the continuity between literal Israel and God's people, "a remnant, chosen by grace" (Romans 11:5, RSV), is clearly indicated in the New Testament. Faithless Jews, on the other hand, are depicted as "hardened" (verse 7, RSV), not constituting the true Israel.

Gentiles, who formerly did not believe, accepted the gospel and were grafted into God's true people, a community made up of believers irrespective of their ethnic origin (Romans 11:13–24). So the Gentiles, "at that time separated from Christ, alienated from the commonwealth of Israel, and strangers to the covenants of promise" (Ephesians 2:12, RSV), were brought near in the blood of Christ and are now "no longer strangers and sojourners, but . . . fellow citizens with the saints and members of the household of God" (verse 19, RSV). Christ is mediating the "new covenant" (Hebrews 9:15, RSV) for all believers, no matter whether they are Jew or Gentile, black or white, yellow or brown, male or female.

The law in both covenants is the same. "Under the new covenant, the conditions by which eternal life may be gained are the same as under the old—perfect obedience."[2] More on this significant element of comparison as we proceed.

New-covenant elements

Readers of the Word of God are always blessed anew as they restudy and reinvestigate the rich passage of Jeremiah 31:31–34. This passage contains basic elements that we would do well to contemplate. It says something about the divine initiative, the human response, the idea of God's law, the purpose of covenanting, and the result of covenanting. Let us briefly consider each of these ideas.

We have noticed already how Jeremiah 31:31–34 repeatedly stresses the divine initiative. This prediction begins with a statement of divine action, "*I will make* a new covenant." Here God announces His saving action that will take place in the future. Likewise, this new-covenant prediction concludes with the words, "I will forgive" and "I will remember their sin no more." This divine initiative aims at the culminating action of God's total forgiveness and total forgetfulness regarding human sins.

The human response also comes through clearly in this significant text. The human response in covenant making cannot be overlooked.

God never reduces human beings to automatons or robots, without the possibility of making choices. The new covenant, like the Sinai covenant, is not an unconditional covenant that remains unbroken generation after generation, regardless of man's response and his relationship to God and to His revealed will in the law. What makes the new covenant permanent and everlasting is that the Lord Himself will work a change in human hearts, making it possible for them to fulfill the law by His divine and enabling grace (Jeremiah 24:7; Ezekiel 36:26–28).

The statement in new-covenant promise about God's law is also of pivotal significance. A common element in the prior covenants made with Adam and Abraham and particularly in the covenant made with ancient Israel on Mount Sinai, is also the law of God. God's law, appropriately called here "my law" (Jeremiah 31:33), was in the Sinai covenant God's law written on tablets of stone (see Exodus 24:12; 31:18; 34:1, 28). The tablets of stone were actually sometimes called "the covenant" (see 1 Kings 8:21). This law of God is not faulty and was not done away with. God's law is immutable and eternal.

Furthermore, this immutable expression of God's will in the law is not to remain external to the believer. For this reason, this new-covenant passage emphasizes that the law will be written by God "upon their hearts." "The great law of love revealed in Eden, proclaimed from Sinai, and in the new covenant written in the heart, is that which binds the human worker to the will of God."[3] This activity of God, in writing His law upon the human heart, is His marvelous work of grace within us. It is His work to write the law inwardly through His Holy Spirit. Thus the law becomes internalized within the believer and will be an integral part of the believer's will, permeating it so as to make the human will and the divine law conform perfectly to each other (2 Corinthians 3:5, 6).

The resulting obedience is not a human achievement, it is not meritorious obedience, it is not obedience aimed at achieving justification and salvation by one's own efforts; it is, rather, faith-obedience, an obedience made possible by faith in the enabling power of Jesus Christ.

The purpose of covenanting is clearly outlined in Jeremiah 31:31–34.

The New Covenant

God does not speak of a new law but of a new covenant. The law as the way of life gives expression to this new-covenant relationship. The relationship is actually expressed by a formula: I "will be their God, and they shall be my people" (Jeremiah 31:33; compare 7:23; 32:38). The covenant relationship of the Sinai covenant was described by the same formula (Exodus 6:7; Deuteronomy 26:16–19; Leviticus 26:12; etc). God's purpose for His people is that this promised relationship, so short-lived for ancient Israel, would be renewed and restored and made permanent.

The results of covenanting are of utmost significance. Chief among these ranks the ensuing experience of the new-covenant community in becoming a spiritual Israel, made up of those who allow God to internalize His law within them and who, thereby, become sanctified channels to enlighten and bless others. The new covenant would also establish a lasting, profound, and deep relationship and communion between the human partners and their covenanting Lord, the God of their salvation. In addition, it would bring the gratifying blessing of forgiveness, which brings peace to mind and soul (Jeremiah 31:34). It would be a forgiveness that would be secured and anchored in the sacrifice of God's own Son.

Newness of the new covenant

In English the opposite of *new* is *old*. The word *old* implies prior existence or continued usage for a long time. It also frequently designates something antiquated in the sense that something has fallen into disuse or is out-of-date. We should be careful not to superimpose modern-day meanings upon biblical usage when it comes to understanding the intent, purpose, and design of biblical language.

The term *new* with regard to the "new covenant" in Jeremiah 31:31 is the Hebrew term *chādāš*. This Hebrew term means frequently (1) "to renew" or "to restore" and (2) something "new" which was not yet present in the same quality or way before. Reflecting both senses, the new covenant is simply a "renewed" or "restored" covenant, also now having characteristics not present in the same way or quality as before.

The apostle Paul in 2 Corinthians 3:6 suggests that the new covenant is a covenant of the Spirit, in contrast to the old covenant, which was a written code: "We serve in newness of the Spirit and not in oldness of the letter" (Romans 7:6, NASB). What Paul seems to be emphasizing here is that the written code (see 2 Corinthians 3:5, 6, RSV) is the letter of the law in the sense of that which is outside of the believer and not yet written within him. As long as the "written code" (simply a designation of the old covenant) remains outside of the believer and not written by the Spirit within him, it can bring only condemnation.

But the Spirit, who characterizes the new covenant, gives life; He writes the law upon the heart and thus internalizes the law within the believer. Thus the newness of the covenant is characterized most effectively by the word "better" (Hebrews 8:6). God's covenant remains or becomes obsolete at the very moment when it remains outside of the human heart, when it is merely a method of law keeping in order to gain salvation by human merit. Paul stresses, in contrast to this approach to salvation—and here he is in complete harmony with a total scriptural emphasis—that the new covenant is a covenant of the Spirit, the believer is now serving in the newness of the Spirit and not in the oldness of the letter (Romans 7:6).

---

1. On the relationship between the old and new covenant, see Michael G. Hasel, "Old and New: Continuity and Discontinuity in God's Everlasting Covenant," *Ministry* 79 no. 3 (March 2007), 18–23.

2. Ellen G. White, "Comments," *Seventh-day Adventist Bible Commentary*, vol. 7 (Hagerstown, MD: Review and Herald®, 1956), 931.

3. Ellen G. White, *The Desire of Ages* (Mountain View, CA: Pacific Press®, 1940), 329.

Eleven

New Covenant Sanctuary and Ministries

The letter to the Hebrews contains a very rich prophetic and typological relationship between the plan of God as revealed through the Hebrew sacrificial system and His plan as revealed through the personal ministry of Jesus Christ in His life, death, ascension, and heavenly mediation.[1] Hebrews 9:15 introduces us to a study of these two complementing revelations of God's plan. "He is the mediator of the new covenant, so that those who are called may receive the promised eternal inheritance, since a death has occurred which redeems them from the transgressions under the first covenant" (RSV).

Here Scripture gives clear emphasis to Jesus Christ as our heavenly Mediator of a superior covenant. He fulfilled the type of the so-called old covenant in a twofold way.

First, He is the true Sacrifice upon which that covenant is based, whose blood also ratified it. Christ's blood also ratified the new covenant and antiquated the Sinai covenant and its mediatorial system built upon animal sacrifices. "The Abrahamic covenant was ratified by the blood of Christ, and it is called the 'second,' or 'new,' covenant, because the blood by which it was sealed was shed after the blood of the first covenant."[2]

Second, Christ fulfilled the type by becoming the Mediator of the new covenant, as Moses was mediator of the Sinai covenant. The mediatorship of Jesus Christ, however, also includes redemption "from the transgressions under the first covenant" (Hebrews 9:15, RSV). This all-inclusiveness indicates that the sacrifices of the Sinai covenant were only types pointing forward to Christ's death on the cross and found their meaning only in the sacrificial, substitutionary death of Christ. His mediatorship, then, must be understood to affect the redemption of all believers, whether under the new covenant or the old.

The new covenant also is superior to the old in the assurance of forgiveness. It would be a mistake, however, to get the impression that under the Sinai covenant, with its animal sacrifices, no forgiveness was available. God's forgiveness was promised to those penitent ones, too, in the period during which the Sinai covenant was functioning (Exodus 34:6, 7; Leviticus 4:20, 26, 31, 35; 19:22; Psalm 103:12; Isaiah 38:17; 43:25; Nehemiah 9:17). But the forgiveness under the Sinai covenant was proleptic or anticipatory of the forgiveness that would be secured by the blood of Christ (Hebrews 9:15), shed "for many for the remission of sins" (Matthew 26:28).

The forgiveness of sin under the new covenant can be called superior in the sense that it is secured in the death of Christ on the cross. In the old covenant, sin was forgiven in view of and in anticipation of what Christ would achieve on the cross when He would die for the sins of humankind; but in the new covenant, forgiveness is bestowed on the basis of what has already been accomplished on the cross. In the first instance, believers looked forward to the accomplishment of the Son of God; in the second, we look back upon what already has been accomplished by Him.

The real sanctuary in heaven

Just as the old covenant had a sanctuary, so the new covenant has a sanctuary. The sanctuary in heaven is not merely an idea in the heavenly world that has a shadowy reflection on earth; rather it is very real—something at the heart of the universe that can be seen and appreciated.[3]

God desired to reside with His people; so He said, "Let them make me a sanctuary, that I may dwell in their midst" (Exodus 25:8, RSV). God's full purpose for the construction of a moveable sanctuary in the wilderness was that He might be more intimately present in the midst of His covenant people. He designed that the earthly sanctuary, erected for the abode of the Divine Presence, should reveal His purpose to make human hearts a temple for His indwelling—a key provision of the new covenant (Hebrews 13:20, 21).[4] The entire process of making the covenant (Exodus 19 and 24) and giving the law (Exodus 20:1–11) stands as the guarantee of the reality of God's presence in His tabernacle and in the hearts of His people.

A careful investigation of Exodus 25:9, 40 reveals that the threefold repetition of the word "pattern" (Hebrew *tabnît*) expresses the idea that Moses in his vision (Numbers 8:4) was shown a scale model or miniature copy of the heavenly sanctuary. God instructed him to build the earthly sanctuary after the pattern of this miniature model. Therefore the earthly sanctuary was a copy patterned after the heavenly reality.[5]

The New Testament book of Revelation clearly emphasizes that the heavenly temple or sanctuary is not to be equated with all heaven. Revelation 11:19 clearly brings to view a temple "in heaven" that was opened and the ark of the covenant within this divine temple. In Revelation 14:17, the revelator reports that "another angel came out of the temple *in* heaven" (RSV; emphasis supplied). This emphasis appears again in Revelation 15:5, where the verse states that "the temple of the tent of witness *in* heaven was opened" (RSV; emphasis supplied). These repeated emphases reveal beyond a doubt that a temple or sanctuary exists in heaven and that in no way can heaven itself or the upper heavens be construed to be the sanctuary. In short, it is clear on the basis of the vision seen by Moses and the vision seen by John the revelator that a sharp distinction must be drawn between heaven itself and God's sanctuary or temple in heaven.

The reality of the heavenly sanctuary also is emphasized in Hebrews 8. In verse 2, we find the adjective "true" associated with the heavenly sanctuary (RSV). The heavenly sanctuary is the "true tent." The word *true* here would be better rendered in the English as *real* because the Greek adjective employed here is *alēthinós*, which stands for "real" as opposed to merely "apparent." (Another Greek adjective, *alēthēs*, does mean "true," and it defines something as "true" as opposed to "false.") This "true tabernacle" (Hebrews 8:2) is the original of which the earthly two-part sanctuary is a "copy and shadow" (Hebrews 8:5, RSV). The earthly sanctuary is but a "shadow"; the reality is in heaven. The "shadow" on earth reflects the real, physical reality of the two-part sanctuary in heaven, which casts the shadow (compare Exodus 25:40; 26:30; 27:8).

The letter to the Hebrews informs us that in the upper heavens (Hebrews 4:14; 7:26; 8:1, 2; 9:24; 12:25, 26), far above the earth and the heavens that will be shaken by God (Hebrews 1:10–12; 11:1, 2; 12:26), there exists the reality of the heavenly Jerusalem (Hebrews 11:10; 12:22; 13:14) and the "real" two-part sanctuary (Hebrews 8:2, 5; 9:11, 28). As its earthly copy had its two compartments (Hebrews 9:1–6), so the heavenly original has two parts or arenas (Hebrews 8:2, 5; 9:8, 11, 12, 23, 24; 10:19), one of which contains the throne of God (Hebrews 4:16; 8:1; 12:2). This real two-part sanctuary in heaven is not only the original but also the very location of Christ's saving, beneficent heavenly ministry.

The logic of the letter to the Hebrews demands that just as the old covenant had a sanctuary with two parts, so the new covenant has a sanctuary with two parts. The typology used in Hebrews 8:1–5 and Hebrews 9:8–28 depicts a vertical, heavenly-earthly typology and an original-copy typology.

Hebrews 9:1–5 describes the structure of the earthly sanctuary with the Holy and Most Holy places. Verses 6 and 7 give details of the respective services. In Hebrews 9:8, the expression "first tent" or "outer tent" (*prōtē skēnē*) is used in the temporal sense of the "first sanctuary" or "former sanctuary" of the old covenant in its entirety, including both the Holy Place and the Most Holy Place.

In Hebrews 9:8, the expression "sanctuary" (RSV) (Greek, *ta hagia*) refers to the entire heavenly sanctuary with its two divisions. "The greater and more perfect tent (not made with hands)" (Hebrews 9:11, RSV) refers, likewise, to the two-part, two-division heavenly sanctuary. All of this affirms that the New Testament as well as the Old (Psalms 1:4; 18:6; 29:9; 60:6; 63:2; 68:35; 96:6; 150:1; Micah 1:2, 3; Habakkuk 2:20; etc.), teach the reality of the heavenly sanctuary and that it is a true or "real" two-part heavenly sanctuary—and not merely an idea or metaphor.

Before the New Testament period, the divinely appointed way for the sinner to rid himself of sin and guilt was through the bringing of animal sacrifices. Leviticus 1–7 details the Israelite sacrificial offerings. Procedures called for careful attention to the use and disposal of the blood in the various kinds of sacrifices.

The person who had sinned had himself broken the covenant relationship and the law that regulated it. This person under the old covenant could be restored into full fellowship with God and his fellow humans if that person would bring an animal as sacrifice to substitute for him. Sacrifices, with their rites, were the God-appointed means to bring about cleansing from sin and guilt. They had been instituted to cleanse the sinner, to transfer the sinner's sin and guilt by blood sprinkling to the sanctuary, and to reinstitute communion and full covenantal fellowship with God and one's fellow human beings. "In fact, the law requires that nearly everything be cleansed with blood, and without the shedding of blood there is no forgiveness" (Hebrews 9:22, NIV).

The perceptive Israelite knew that the animal sacrifices were God's appointed means of prophetically pointing forward to the great Sacrifice. An animal certainly could not substitute as an adequate atonement for a person's sin and guilt (see Hosea 6:6; Psalms 50:8–15; 51:15–19; Isaiah 1:10–18; 53). The author of Hebrews states explicitly, "It is impossible that the blood of bulls and goats should take away sins" (Hebrews 10:4, RSV). Thus animal sacrifice was but an anticipatory prefiguration of the Sacrifice to come, who would die a substitutionary death for the sins of the world.

This profound truth is expressed prophetically in one of the most majestic chapters in all of Scripture:

He was pierced through for our transgressions,

He was crushed for our iniquities;

The chastening of our well-being fell upon Him,

And by His scourging we were healed.

All of us like sheep have gone astray,
Each of us has turned to his own way;
But the LORD has caused the iniquity of us all
To fall on Him.
He was oppressed and He was afflicted,
Yet He did not open His mouth;
Like a lamb that is led to the slaughter,
And like a sheep that is silent before its shearers,
So He did not open His mouth (Isaiah 53:5–7, NASB).

These prophetic words about the coming Messiah and His place as the Sacrifice manifest God's beautiful plan for the salvation of humanity.

The fact that Jesus Christ died on the cross as a sacrifice is the major theme of the New Testament. Jesus is spoken of as the Lamb of God slain vicariously: "Behold, the Lamb of God, who takes away the sin of the world!" (John 1:29, RSV). Paul describes Jesus as the "paschal lamb" that has been "sacrificed" (1 Corinthians 5:7, RSV). Indeed, Jesus Christ "gave himself up for us" as a "sacrifice to God" (Ephesians 5:2, RSV), "like that of a lamb without blemish or spot" (1 Peter 1:19, RSV). He "offered for all time a single sacrifice for sins" (Hebrews 10:12, RSV).

The idea that Christ's death on the cross was substitutionary and not merely representative has fallen out of favor with many interpreters.[6] Yet the substitutionary death of Christ on the cross cannot easily be denied. The New Testament insists time and again that Christ, who Himself lived "without sin" (Hebrews 4:15), died "for" sin (Romans 8:3) and was crucified for men and women. Christ "gave himself for our sins" (Galatians 1:4). He "was put to death for our trespasses" (Romans 4:25, RSV). He "died for our sins according to the scriptures" (1 Corinthians 15:3). These passages, together with Galatians 3:13 and 2 Corinthians 5:14, demonstrate that Christ's death on the cross was substitutionary. He did die in our place. He substituted Himself for us. He died the death of the transgressor, paying the penalty for our sin, thereby providing life and fellowship with Himself and the Godhead forever.[7]

Just as the animal was killed at the altar outside of the sanctuary, so Jesus Christ died on the cross on earth outside of the heavenly sanctuary. Christ's death on the cross summed up and fulfilled all the types and shadows in all the various sacrifices in the Old Testament system, which all pointed forward to His death.

When Jesus Christ died on the cross, the temple and its ritual lost their significance. The curtain in the temple was torn in half (Matthew 27:51), indicating that the temple and its services had now lost their meaning in God's plan. Even though the Jews—and even certain Hebrew Christians, as we can gather from the letter to the Hebrews—continued to offer sacrifices in the earthly temple, these sacrifices were to no avail. Jesus Christ, the real Sacrifice, had come, fulfilling the totality of what these animal sacrifices had pointed forward to, making such sacrifices meaningless after He had died.

The first phase of Christ's heavenly ministry

After the dedication of the earthly sanctuary (Exodus 40:1–11) and the installation of the priests (Exodus 40:12–15; 30:30–33), the ministry in the earthly sanctuary was inaugurated. Antitypically, our heavenly Priest and High Priest also began His ministry in the heavenly sanctuary after its dedication, a service predicted in Daniel 9:24. The Pentecostal outpouring of the Holy Spirit signified, according to Acts 2:33, that Christ had been installed in His heavenly ministry. By means of the Holy Spirit, the ministering Christ sustains His church on earth and vindicates believers before their enemies.

Jesus is our heavenly "mediator" of a superior covenant. Christ's own blood, shed on Calvary on our behalf, ratified the new covenant and antiquated the prior covenant and its mediatorial system. Christ's own blood gives us "confidence to enter the sanctuary" (Hebrews 10:19, RSV). It provides the "new and living way" (verse 20, RSV) through which we can "with confidence draw near to the throne of grace" (Hebrews 4:16, RSV).

Christ is our heavenly Priest and High Priest. The designation "priest" is applied three times in the letter to the Hebrews to the exalted and enthroned Christ (Hebrews 7:15; 8:4; 10:21). In Hebrews 7:15, 16, Christ is presented as the Royal Priest after the order of Melchizedek. Melchizedek, never called a "high priest" but rather a "priest," stands as a type of Christ, the heavenly "priest."

Another special mark of the letter to the Hebrews is the development of an extensive typology of Christ as heavenly High Priest. Careful recent investigations of this typology show it to have both horizontal and vertical aspects. We spoke earlier of vertical typology. The high-priestly typology of Hebrews is developed primarily along horizontal lines. Hebrews 5:4, 5, emphasizes that Jesus was called by God to His high-priestly office just as Aaron was. His appointment was a fulfillment of the prediction recorded in Psalm 110:4. Christ was "designated" (Hebrews 5:10, RSV) and "exalted above the heavens" (Hebrews 7:26, RSV). His appointment as heavenly High Priest came as a result of a divine call and not through an act of self-appointment or through physical inheritance. Thus invested, Christ demonstrates His high-priestly and priestly ministries to be of a superior nature.

The New Testament depicts Christ's function in heaven, aside from that of Priest and High Priest, as also that of Mediator and Intercessor. Paul depicts Moses as the "mediator" of the law (Galatians 3:19); but in 1 Timothy 2:5, the Lord Jesus Christ, who gave Himself as a ransom for all, is designated the "one mediator between God and men." The term *Mediator* is one of the great New Testament titles for Jesus and is applied to Him four times in the New Testament: 1 Timothy 2:5; Hebrews 8:6; 9:15; and 12:24.

A "mediator" in the New Testament use of the word is an arbiter or intermediary whose task it is to bring together two estranged parties. He writes out the differences between the estranged parties and also inaugurates a contract or a covenant. A "mediator" also may serve as a guarantor or surety (Hebrews 7:22) who takes over the debt of another person.

Thus in the first phase of Christ's heavenly ministry, carried on in the first part or arena of the heavenly sanctuary, the heavenly Mediator, Jesus, acts as Intermediary between us and God. He is the connecting link between God and humanity. He, as our Mediator, has paid all debts of each of His clients. Jesus is the Mediator who stands good for our debt to God because of that which is represented by His blood (Hebrews 10:10, 19), having given Himself for us. He alone is able to bring together the two estranged parties.

Jesus Christ is the way of access into the heavenly sanctuary (see Hebrews 9:8). His ongoing mediation in the heavenly sanctuary is so perfect and of such a superior nature that the believer in Christ needs no other mediator, whether on earth or in heaven. The unique glory of Christ as Mediator demands that the faithful not invest any other being with even a semblance of the function and work that Jesus Christ is performing in the heavenly sanctuary.

Christ also functions as heavenly Intercessor. Christ's heavenly ministry includes the aspect of a "standing intercession," this mediation being stressed in the form of the verb in Romans 8:34. Jesus also is said to "make intercession for" those "who draw near to God through him" (Hebrews 7:25, RSV). The teaching of Christ's continuous heavenly intercession is most fully developed in the letter to the Hebrews, where His intercessory activities are shown to be continuously carried on (Hebrews 7:25) "in the presence of God on our behalf" (Hebrews 9:24, RSV), where they will be continued as long as Christ is High Priest (Hebrews 6:20; 7:3).

This intercession, carried on for each one who draws near to God through Christ, is a genuine high-priestly act. Through His intercessory function, our heavenly High Priest cleanses us from all unrighteousness. Christ's intercessory function is that of a *Paraclete*, an Advocate with the Father (1 John 2:1), who speaks to the Father in our defense, in order that the confessed sins of the saints may be forgiven.

The knowledge of Christ's function as intermediary and intercessory Priest and High Priest in heaven, as our heavenly Mediator and Intercessor, makes us confident of our salvation. It sets us free from guilt as we confess our sins to Him. It lifts us up to a high plane of spiritual growth.

It teaches us of Him through whom alone we can become perfect. Our knowledge of Christ's heavenly function provides an essential key to the meaning of righteousness by faith.

The second phase of Christ's heavenly ministry

The second phase of Christ's heavenly ministry in the second division or arena of the heavenly sanctuary began in 1844. The separation of this second phase of Christ's heavenly ministry from the first is typologically related to the separation of the earthly ministry of the high priest on the Day of Atonement from that carried on daily by the priests throughout the year. The "yearly" ministry of the earthly high priest during Old Testament times on the great Day of Atonement corresponds typologically to the second phase of Christ's ministry in the second division of the heavenly sanctuary.

In examining the second phase of Christ's sanctuary ministry in heaven, it is of great importance to recognize that the second phase does not do away with the first phase. To the contrary, a new, second phase of ministry is added to the first phase so that both phases continue to operate simultaneously. We see the parallel in the earthly sanctuary service. On the great Day of Atonement, a continual burnt offering was offered that day also, aside from the special sacrifices of that day (Numbers 29:11). Likewise, at the commencement of the second phase of Christ's atoning ministry, the High-Priestly phase, He did not cease to function as Intercessor and Mediator. During the second phase, as well as during the first, forgiveness as well as the other benefits that accrue to the believer from Christ's priestly ministry continue to be available.

Now we will examine the time factor in the comparison of the typical priestly ministry with the antitypical. The judgment scene in Daniel 7 illuminates this aspect of the subject. It is set within the temporal framework of the time of the end—after the 1,260-day/year prophecy of little-horn domination over the people of God has been fulfilled and before the people of God will receive the kingdom (Daniel 7:21, 22). Further amplification about aspects of the subject already revealed in the vision of Daniel 7 is found in Daniel 8:13, 14. Specifically, it provides details regarding the time element of the second phase, referring to the second phase as the "cleansing" of the heavenly sanctuary and dating it as commencing when the 2,300 years are concluded, namely, in 1844. (See Daniel 9:24–27 for the reasons why the 2,300-year/day prophecy began in 457 BC.)

It is stunning to note that the term *sanctuary* in Daniel 8:14 is the Hebrew term *qōdesh*. This very term is the typical term used to designate the sanctuary ("tent of meeting," "holy place," etc.) to be cleansed on the Day of Atonement in Leviticus 16, where it appears eight times (verses 2, 3, 16, 17, 20, 23, 27, 33). It clearly demonstrates a link in terminology as well as concept between Daniel 8:14 and Leviticus 16. In Leviticus 16, the chapter on the great Day of Atonement, the cleansing of the sanctuary is that of the old covenant. But in Daniel 8:14, the "cleansing" of the sanctuary is that of the new covenant, the sanctuary anointed after Christ's death and ascension (see Daniel 9:24, last phrase) and now being cleansed in the "time of the end" (Daniel 8:17; compare verse 19).

Described in Daniel 8:14, the activity to take place in the heavenly sanctuary is one for which Daniel used a word traditionally translated into English as "cleansed." The Hebrew term is *nisdaq*, the only use of this verbal form in the Old Testament. It has been translated "cleansed" from the earliest period of translations in other languages. Two Greek translations called the Septuagint and Theodotian contain the same translation "cleansed." In the Latin translation known as the Vulgate, the word is translated *mundabitur*, "cleaned" or "purified." This is true also of the ancient Syriac and Coptic translations.

Careful philological investigation reveals that the idea of "cleansed" is part of the connotation of this term, as parallel Hebrew terms (Job 4:17; 17:9; 15:14; Psalm 51:7; Proverbs 20:7–9) that mean "cleanse" or "purify" in the Hebrew language indicate. But the Hebrew term *nisdaq* in Daniel 8:14 also encompasses such ideas as "setting right" or "restoring" as well as "justifying" and "vindicating."[8] There seems to be no adequate English term that would capture in one word the various ranges of meaning, such as cleansing, setting right, justifying, and vindicating, that need to be encapsulated in a single term to convey the richness of this Hebrew word.

We have pointed out earlier that the new phase in Christ's heavenly ministry began in the year 1844, an activity in the second part or arena of the heavenly sanctuary. This pre-Advent activity is the antitype of the Day of Atonement work in the Levitical system. It is carried on in the Most Holy Place of the heavenly sanctuary and has cosmic dimensions. The "cleansing" involves the blotting out of sin. The "setting right" or "restoring" involves gaining the proper place for the function of Christ's high-priestly intercession during this last phase of His heavenly ministry. The "justifying" involves judicial-forensic judgment activity, in which decision is rendered about those who will be raised to life and those to be rescued at the Second Coming (see Daniel 12:1–3). The "vindicating" involves the saints being cleared before the intelligences of the universe (see Daniel 7:9, 10) and accounted worthy of citizenship in the eternal kingdom of God. The "vindicating" also involves God's character and justice being vindicated.

The judicial-redemptive-cleansing activity described in Daniel 8:14 pinpoints precisely the beginning of these events in the celestial sanctuary—they take place at the end of the 2,300 "evenings and mornings." These celestial activities are compared with the typical Day of Atonement activities reported in Leviticus 16—the cleansing, setting right, justifying, and vindicating of both sanctuary and saints. This judicial-redemptive-cleansing end-time activity before the intelligences of the universe restores the sanctuary to its rightful place, causes sins to be blotted out and that the saints, as well as God Himself, are vindicated before the universe.

The covenanted basis of the judicial-redemptive-cleansing activity in the heavenly sanctuary for the people of God is Christ and His sacrifice— "Michael, the great prince who has charge of your people" (Daniel 12:1, RSV; compare Jude 9). He is able to come forth victoriously in the time of trouble and physically deliver the saints, "every one whose name shall be found written in the book. And many of those who sleep in the dust of the earth shall awake, some to everlasting life, and some to shame and everlasting contempt" (Daniel 12:1, 2, RSV). Evidently the grand climax of the judicial-redemptive-cleansing, end-time activity (justification, cleansing, vindication, restoration) affects both the heavenly sanctuary and the earthly saints.

A contemplation of this majestic, marvelous, and mind-stretching work of Jesus Christ can reveal to each of us a true sense of the lofty privilege of belonging to God's people in a covenant relationship. We are not alone in our struggles. Rather, our heavenly High Priest now assures us of His ministry for us above and His presence with us and in us here below. Contemplation of what is going on in heaven in our behalf also invites and motivates us to participate in a personal cleansing of our lives by His grace. Further, a genuine understanding of the heavenly activity being carried on in the Most Holy part of the heavenly sanctuary should spur us with a sense of mission to cooperate with Him in getting people ready for His return.

---

1. See articles in Frank B. Holbrook, ed., *Issues in the Book of Hebrews*, Daniel and Revelation Committee Series, 4 (Silver Spring, MD: Biblical Research Institute, 1989).

2. Ellen G. White, *Patriarchs and Prophets* (Mountain View, CA: Pacific Press®, 1958), 371.

3. William G. Johnsson, "The Heavenly Sanctuary: Figurative or Real?" *Issues in the Book of Hebrews*, 35–51; cf. Angel Manuel Rodríguez, "The Sanctuary," *Handbook of Seventh-day Adventist Theology*, Commentary Reference Series, ed., Raoul Dederen (Hagerstown, MD: Review and Herald®, 2000), 388, 389, 412–416.

4. Ellen G. White, *The Desire of Ages* (Mountain View, CA: Pacific Press®, 1940), 161.

5. Rodríguez, "Sanctuary," 381, 382.

6. See the convenient survey by Richard Rice, "The Doctrine of Atonement in Contemporary Protestant Theology," *The Sanctuary and the Atonement: Biblical, Historical, and Theological Studies*, eds., Arnold V. Wallenkampf and W. Richard Lesher (Washington, DC: Review and Herald®, 1981), 478–499.

7. Raoul Dederen, "Christ: His Person and Work," *Handbook*, 175–182; Rodríguez, "Salvation by Sacrificial Substitution," *Journal of the Adventist Theological Society* 3/2 (1992): 49–77.

8. Gerhard F. Hasel, "The 'Little Horn,' the Heavenly Sanctuary and the Time of the End: A Study of Daniel 8:9–14," *Symposium on Daniel*, ed., Frank B. Holbrook (Washington DC: Biblical Research Institute, 1986), 448–461; Richard M. Davidson, "The Meaning of *Nisdaq* in Daniel 8:14," *Journal of the Adventist Theological Society* 7/1 (1996): 107–119.

Twelve

Covenant and Faith: Reckoned as Righteousness

Abraham is the Bible's hero of faith (Hebrews 11:8–12; Romans 4). He is also "the Friend of God" (James 2:23). Abraham fascinates every student of the Word of God. One of the most fantastic sentences in the entire Bible refers to Abraham's life experience recorded in Genesis 15:6: "He believed in Jehovah; and he reckoned it to him for righteousness" (ARV).

Those who have read this sentence and contemplated it keep wondering what the idea behind the clause "he believed in Jehovah" indicates. What does it mean to believe in the Lord? What does it mean "to reckon" something as righteousness? What does "righteousness" mean in a context in which both "reckoned" and "believed" appear? These and other questions come to mind as one contemplates this remarkable sentence.

Friend of God

As we study this important passage in Genesis 15:6, it will be helpful to keep in mind that it comes within the context of God making a covenant with Abraham. The Lord addressed Abraham in the vision recorded in Genesis 15:1 as follows: "Fear not, Abram, I am your shield; your reward shall be very great" (RSV). It was a revelation of divine origin.

Covenant and Faith: Reckoned as Righteousness

The introductory words, "Fear not," presented a challenge designed to arouse faith. Here Abraham faced a test to have faith and trust in (1) the person of God ("I am your shield") and (2) in His promise ("your reward shall be very great").

Abraham demurred with a spirited response, "O Lord GOD, what wilt thou give me, for I continue childless, and the heir of my house is Eliezer of Damascus?" (Genesis 15:2, RSV). Abraham here questioned God about His promises. He was quite willing to substitute the head servant of his household for an authentic son. But the Lord insisted that one born from Abraham's own loins should be his heir, despite Abraham's and Sarah's inability to produce an heir.

To Abraham, it seemed that God had been slack in fulfilling His promises. So Abraham questioned God, not simply out of curiosity but with an honest inquiry regarding the fulfillment of the promise. The promise of offspring seemed no nearer fulfillment at this time than when God had first assured him that his seed would inherit the land. Now nearly an octogenarian, Abraham had lost hope that he would ever have an heir, a son of his own.

God planned for Abraham to have a natural son, not an adopted one. So God spoke to him a second time: "This man shall not be your heir; your own son shall be your heir" (verse 4, RSV). This additional promise hardly made faith easier for Abraham. He and Sarah had had years of disappointment over her barrenness, and now they had grown old. Abraham could not see how he could have a natural son.

At this point God requested that Abraham go outside the tent and look at the countless stars. Everyone who has gazed up into the heavens on a starry night recognizes their place in the order of the universe—a mere speck in the vast expanse of God's creation. Our problems are suddenly diminished, for we recognize that God is all-powerful and omniscient. God presents this reassurance to Abraham; but He has a greater purpose. The Lord God says, "Look up at the heavens and count the stars—if indeed you can count them. . . . So shall your offspring be" (Genesis 15:5, NIV).

What was God doing here? How was this command to look at the starry night sky to give Abraham assurance that God would indeed fulfill His promise? How much comfort was there in looking at the stars? He had previously seen them time and again, and they had meant nothing special to him. But now, with God using them as an illustration, the stars did make the promise vivid, although they were not assuring in themselves. What was assuring and confirming was the specific "word of the Lord." The starry sky did not make the difference. The difference for Abraham was the divine word of promise. This word was sufficient for him. "And he believed in the LORD" (verse 6, NIV).

Faith in the Lord

Let us first notice that this is the earliest statement in the Bible to mention faith. Before Genesis 15:6, the noun *faith* or the verb *to believe* have not yet appeared in the Pentateuch.

The form of the verb *to believe* that appears here comes from the Hebrew term *he'-mîn*. This term is normally translated "to believe" but can also be rendered "to have faith." It is noteworthy that when the Bible speaks explicitly for the first time about faith, it puts it in a context of "faith in the Lord." And the Lord reckons this faith as righteousness to the one who manifests it.

Let us pursue further the nature of the faith first mentioned in the Bible. To begin with, note what it is not. Faith in Genesis 15:6 is not a crowning merit on the part of Abraham. Faith here is not intellectual assent to a fixed body of truth. Notice that Genesis 15:6 does not say, "Abraham believed *this* of the Lord." Instead, the text states definitely that "Abraham believed in the LORD."

Do you notice that we have consistently departed from some customary English translations of Genesis 15:6? The translation common in many English versions is, "Abraham believed the LORD." But the Hebrew text has a preposition following the verb, that translates into English as the preposition *in*. Several English versions include the preposition and translate the sentence exactly: "He believed in the LORD."

Distinction between "he believed" and "he believed in" can be found elsewhere in the books of Moses. In Genesis 45:26, Jacob does not believe his sons when they tell him that Joseph is still alive. In Exodus 4:1, 8, 9, God gives Moses power to perform signs because the Israelites may not believe him. Moses does not anticipate that the Israelites will believe *in* him; but that the signs will cause them to believe him, as they then are said to have done (verse 31). Later in Moses' career, the Israelites are said to have believed in him (Exodus 14:31). The fact is that "to believe in" is much more comprehensive as an idea than merely "to believe."

What brought about this faith response in Abraham? It was brought about by the divine initiative. It was brought about by the Lord. He appeared to Abraham in a revelatory event in history. The Lord, or Yahweh, the God who guides human beings and who is the sovereign over history and directs it, had come again to Abraham. So Abraham's faith was faith *in* a Person, the Divine Being. Thus this faith and trust was "in the LORD."

The second aspect of this covenant experience also has significance. Abraham's faith was a response not only to the appearance of the person Himself but also to a divine promise. We already noted that the starry sky itself did not confirm that Abraham would have a son. The divine word of promise made the difference for Abraham. Faith here means that Abraham fully and unconditionally accepted as sufficient the divine revelation in the form of the promise of a son. This faith responds to a divine revelation that is propositional. It is a tangible promise to be fulfilled in the future. Faith in this instance, as always when it relates to true faith, is evoked by God.

Reckoning

The second major idea in this incredible revelation in Genesis 15:6 is the statement that God "reckoned it to him as righteousness" (RSV). We are particularly interested in the word "reckoned," also translated "credited" (NAB, NIV) or "counted" (NEB, *Jerusalem Bible*) or "accounted" (MLB). The Hebrew term translated by any of these renderings into

English is *chāšab*. This term appears a number of times in the Old Testament, so we can investigate its meaning in other contexts (see, for example, Genesis 31:15; Numbers 18:27, 30; and Leviticus 7:18). God is accounting or regarding the sinner as righteous, although, in a particular sense, he actually is unrighteous. In the divinely given sacrificial law, the declaration that the sacrifice is "reckoned" (or "accounted," etc.) to the sinner follows after the act of sacrifice engaged in by the sinner. In Leviticus 17:1–4, the law commands that an animal be brought to the entrance of the holy tent of meeting to be slaughtered. If, instead, the offering is slaughtered outside the camp and not at the doorway of the tent of meeting, then "bloodguiltiness is to be reckoned ["imputed," RSV] to that man" (verse 4, NASB). Evidently the verb "to reckon" is employed in connection with sacrifices that are acceptable to the Lord. But if sacrifices are not brought in the right way, then these sacrifices cannot be reckoned to the benefit of the one who brings them. Evidently, the priest makes a judgment in behalf of the Lord and declares the offering to be acceptable to the Lord; and so the sacrifice is "reckoned" to the offerer, who now stands again in the right relationship and covenantal communion with God.

Profound insights can be gained from the way the same word is used in various contexts. In Genesis 15:6, it is not a sacrifice being "reckoned" as righteousness but an act of faith evoked by God's initiative. It can hardly be overemphasized that God's act of "reckoning" someone as righteous in His sight is based on that person's faith and not on his sacrifice. In other words, being counted as righteous is not based on an act by a human being but rather upon faith evoked by God Himself within that human being.

Faith-righteousness
In the promise, "He believed in the LORD; and he counted it to him for righteousness" (Genesis 15:6), the last word we need to examine is the pivotal term "righteousness." This term appears in the Old Testament scores of times in various settings and with various meanings. In

English, the term is customarily translated from the underlying Hebrew term *sᵉdāqāh*.

"Righteousness" is not a reward that God pays for faithful service or for obedience. Righteousness does not depend upon some exemplary act of human effort designed to earn merit. God's clearly stated declaration indicates that obedience is not the basis for righteousness. Righteousness is something that God declares to be reckoned to Abraham.

In Abraham's situation, God's use of the term *righteousness* expresses the fact that Abraham is "right" before God. He has a right standing before his Lord. His response of faith to God's word of promise causes God to reckon this faith to Abraham as righteousness. Are we then to conclude that to believe or to have faith is an act of merit? Not at all. "Faith is the condition upon which God has seen fit to promise pardon to sinners; *not that there is any virtue in faith whereby salvation is merited*, but because faith can lay hold of the merits of Christ, the remedy provided for sin."[1] No, faith itself is not a merit. Why is it then that God should reckon this faith of the patriarch Abraham for righteousness? The issue is profound. What qualification resides in simple trust that enables God to attribute to Abraham the experience of righteousness?

The context of Genesis 15:6 requires further consideration as we try to understand how Abraham's faith could be reckoned as righteousness. Abraham believed God's word that a "seed" would be provided from his own loins. He trusted that God would fulfill His promise. He simply trusted God. Abraham's implicit trust in God as a Person and in God's promise reveals that in this particular passage, righteousness describes a relationship. Righteousness, therefore, is reckoned to a person when a right faith relationship exists between him and God. All the while, this faith relationship is not human-produced; it is God-produced and accepted by men and women.

The faith relationship that comes to expression here is found within the covenantal relationship. We find that the verses following Genesis 15:6 record God's covenant-making ceremony with Abraham. This covenant-making in Genesis 15:7–15 was made possible because Abraham was now in the right faith relationship with God. The person who enters this kind of covenant relationship of faith affirms God's promises and God's commands. In other words, he affirms the divine promise (Genesis 15:1–6; Psalm 106:12), and he also affirms the ensuing regulations, or rules of conduct, that express this genuine faith relationship.

The inward relationship of faith in God revealed in Genesis 15:6 must not be equated with passive receptivity. The human dimension of faith and trust and confidence in the promise of the Lord and in the Lord Himself means a submission of one's entire life, present and future, into God's hands. Genuine biblical faith becomes evident in lifestyle and attitudes.

The Ninevites illustrate this submission. When they heard God's message through the prophet Jonah, they "believed in God; and they called a fast and put on sackcloth from the greatest to the least of them" (Jonah 3:5, NASB). Genuine faith in God effects repentance and conversion. Faith in God effected for Abraham his consent to continue following God's plan in history and not to take matters into his own hands. For Abraham to follow God's plan ultimately meant obedience to the point of sacrificing his only son (Genesis 22). The act of Abrahamic faith is placing oneself in God's hands without reservations or conditions and being directed by His wisdom and governed by His laws.

Faith of the kind Abraham manifested provides security in the Lord, the Lord of the covenant, the Lord who evokes faith within the one who listens. Abrahamic faith is faith reckoned as righteousness. It is security in the Lord. The biblical goal of this kind of faith, however, transcends security to praise. The psalmist expresses this point vividly: "Then they believed his promises and sang his praise" (Psalm 106:12, NIV). Faith reckoned as righteousness finds security in the Lord; such faith grounds one's entire life and existence in the covenant God, and it praises Him—even in song.

---

1. Ellen G. White, *Faith and Works* (Washington, DC: Review and Herald®, 1979), 100, 101 (emphasis supplied).

Thirteen

Life, Hope, and the Future

The basic scriptural concept about Jesus Christ as Savior is summed up in His significant statement about Himself: "I am come that they might have life, and that they might have it more abundantly" (John 10:10). Life, real life, adds up to much more than mere physical existence. The great quest to understand the meaning of life in its fullest sense has taken many forms over long centuries of contemplation, study, and investigation. *The New Encyclopaedia Britannica* states flatly: "There is no generally accepted definition of life."[1] Eighteen years later, the authoritative *Encyclopedia Americana* begins its article with this disclaimer: "The greater mankind's knowledge becomes, the harder it is to define the idea of life."[2]

Definitions of *life* may be diverse, but the fact remains undisputed that all known life on planet Earth ends in death. From time immemorial humans have responded to the fact of death by attempting to prepare for their continued existence in an afterlife or by attempting to achieve the richest and fullest life in the here and now. The Egyptian pyramids, for example, stand as evidence of human attempts to guarantee life in the hereafter.

However, all quests to improve or perpetuate life are doomed to fail unless human beings accept the life that God alone can provide, as described in Scripture. Christ's pronouncement, "I am come that they might have life, and that they might have it more abundantly" (John 10:10), sums up the divine answer to the human quest for life at its best.

New-covenant salvation

The apostle Peter makes the astonishing claim that only in Jesus Christ can we find salvation. "There is salvation in no one else; for there is no other name under heaven that has been given among men, by which we must be saved" (Acts 4:12, NASB). Jesus Christ is the grand focal point of salvation.

God's revelation in Scripture about salvation as centered and focused in Jesus Christ runs counter to all humanly devised ways of salvation. Some attempt to understand salvation by wisdom or right knowledge. Gnosticism, a religious and philosophic movement widespread in the first three centuries of the Christian era, taught this method. The diverse teachers, groups, and systems lumped together under the gnostic label share the conviction that, although humankind exists in ignorance and illusion, we can through "knowledge" or "wisdom" attain to spiritual liberation. That is, we may achieve ultimate identity with the divine, whatever that means.[3]

This gnostic philosophy closely parallels the teachings of pagan and nonpagan mysticism. This system of thought concerns the interior life of the spirit, the pilgrimage with the divine, which begins with inner awareness and proceeds to the highest possible stages of personal development. Immediate relation with the ultimate is the essence of its teachings. This relation may be a psychological or an epistemological experience in which the mystic, apart from a religious institution or apart from a sacred book, has religious knowledge directly from the divine.

The biblical teaching of salvation in Jesus Christ also runs counter to legalistic claims to righteousness and salvation. The term *legalism* designates a way of seeking salvation through abiding by rules, regulations, and laws, both human and divine, in order to gain merit in God's sight and to place Him under obligation to grant salvation. Legalism has taken many forms over the centuries, even within Christianity itself. The biblical truth about salvation runs counter to any legalistic method of gaining salvation by religious ritual or acts of contrition.

The way of salvation in Scripture also opposes any form of antinomianism. The antinomian rejects the moral law and right living as an indispensable part of Christian experience, a perversion of truth dating back to New Testament times. Paul, in his day, had to refute the suggestion that the doctrine of justification by faith left room for ongoing indulgence in sin. The Epistles frequently condemn the heresy that the gospel condones licentiousness. In many instances, modern-day discussions about law and grace are really about the necessity of righteous living. Incredibly, the apparent dichotomy between law and grace and the sharp contrast often made between the two stem from a misunderstanding of the teaching of Paul himself. No one, of course, more clearly rejects the law as a means of salvation but simultaneously affirms the continuing validity of the law as an integral component in the Christian's life (see Romans 3:31; 8:4).

The new-covenant salvation comes down to us from the Garden of Eden, designed by God Himself for all of humankind. The entire Bible gives witness to it and about it. It is a salvation grounded in and accomplished by Jesus Christ.

New-covenant life

The new-covenant life is characterized by Christ's life and existence in the believer's heart, the term *heart* used here to designate the seat of thought, purpose, and understanding, from which our attitude, revealed by our behavior, springs. The "stony" heart (Ezekiel 11:19; 36:26), which is also called the "uncircumcised" heart (Ezekiel 44:7), stands in need of re-creation as well as of cleansing (Psalm 51:10; Jeremiah 24:7; Ezekiel 18:31).

Jesus promised that the pure in heart shall see God (Matthew 5:8). The new-covenant promise is that God will write His law into our hearts

(Jeremiah 31:33; Hebrews 10:16, 17). This internalization of the law of God in the believers' hearts makes it possible for them to live the new life of the covenant.

Faith is the means by which Christ dwells in human hearts (Ephesians 3:17), a faith that elicits a response of loving obedience to Christ's words (John 14:23). Christ then becomes a constant and abiding Presence in the believers' hearts, not just an occasional Visitor. He makes a living, covenantal relationship a lasting and continuous reality in the lives of His followers.

The inspired writers of Scripture argue forcefully that a Christian moves on to maturity in Christian life. This maturity involves "repentance from dead works" (Hebrews 6:1, RSV). The letter to the Hebrews raises the following decisive question: "How much more will the blood of Christ, who through the eternal Spirit offered Himself without blemish to God, cleanse your conscience from dead works to serve the living God?" (Hebrews 9:14, NASB).

These "dead works" are not sins leading to death but human works that lack the element that would make them faith-works. They are works produced not out of faith-obedience but, rather, out of a legalistic spirit. In this sense, "dead works" are "works of law"—or works that seek a law-righteousness instead of a faith-righteousness. The way of life characterized by true Christians who live in a genuine and dynamic relationship with Jesus Christ is not one of work-righteousness but one of faith-righteousness. Those who serve the living God bring forth "righteousness and peace and joy in the Holy Spirit" (Romans 14:17, RSV).

New-covenant hope

There are various kinds of hope: national hopes, political hopes, philosophical hopes, theological hopes. These hopes share the common framework of desire accompanied by expectation. The aspect of expectation causes us to raise the question time and again: Is this or that hope free from illusion?

Often, the hopes not based on biblical promises are revealed to be mere projections of human and earthly desires. They paint pictures of the future based on humankind's own wishes. Some of them promise earthly utopia; but dreams of a perfect political society turn out to be mirages. Schemes aiming at perfection fizzle because of the innate imperfection of the schemers. Dreams of riches or fame never materialize. Such hopes and anticipations usually end in failure and disappointment because they are based only on human ability and determination.

The Bible clearly reveals the existence of a hope that is based on reality and not illusion—"a sure and steadfast anchor of the soul" (Hebrews 6:19, RSV). This hope, founded on God's transcendently certain promises, is grounded in God's revelation and revealed through His covenant. This kind of hope is a hope without illusion and a hope without fear of failure.

The emphasis of the Scriptures on hope is the same in both the Old and New Testaments. True hope, the biblical hope, the hope not based on illusion, has God as its Source and Author. The psalmist confesses in Psalm 71:5, "Thou art my hope, O Lord." The prophet Jeremiah twice describes God as the hope of Israel (Jeremiah 14:8; 17:13). God's covenant people base their hope on the Lord of hope. Paul reechoes this theme by calling God "the God of hope" (Romans 15:13).

God is the Author and Source of hope for the believer. He also is the Giver of hope. He gives a hope that reaches forward to the future and will never be disappointed. The psalmist reveals that hope is a gift: "My hope is from Him" (Psalm 62:5, NASB). Paul affirms that the Father has given us "good hope" (2 Thessalonians 2:16). This "good hope" from the Father is totally set apart from hope grounded in human projections, desires, or wishes. In the hope that God provides, desires and expectations are built on Him and nothing else. God Himself guarantees this hope to be without illusion.

A chief aspect of true hope is its promise of eternal life. The New Testament reveals much about eternal life. Eternal life, according to a number of passages in the New Testament, begins in the present. The believer experiences in the present the abundant life (John 10:10; compare

6:33, 35, 63). The quality of eternity resides in Jesus Christ (John 5:26; compare 4:10, 14; 11:25; 14:6); and the believer who continues to partake of Him and who has Jesus Christ living within him "shall live for ever" (John 6:51). In other words, the disciple of Jesus, the one who follows Christ in a daily and dynamic relationship of total submission, experiences eternal life to a degree even now and will never eternally perish (John 10:28).

Then, of course, the future aspect of eternal life involves the resurrection of the body (John 5:28, 29; 6:39, 40, 44, 51–56). Eternal life in this sense clearly consists of a future event and experience. The life characterized as spiritual and not fleshly (compare Romans 8:14; Galatians 5:16) will continue following the resurrection of the body (1 Corinthians 15:44, 51; 2 Corinthians 5:1–5; Philippians 3:21; 1 Thessalonians 4:13–18) at the second coming of the Lord Jesus Christ (1 Corinthians 15:22; Colossians 3:4).

The "now" of salvation is a present reality for the believer. But there remains a "not yet" of salvation still to be realized. Hope in the Old Testament looked forward to the coming of the Messiah, who came as predicted. The "now" of salvation thus became secure through the death-resurrection-ascension aspect of Jesus Christ's ministry; but the "not yet" aspect of salvation's hope is yet to be fulfilled.

The New Testament scriptures express this "not yet" aspect of our hope in a variety of ways. Our hope has a future object. Notice how this aspect is expressed in a number of biblical phrases: "We rejoice in our hope of sharing the glory of God" (Romans 5:2, RSV). We hope for the "redemption of our bodies" (Romans 8:23, RSV). "By faith, we wait for the hope of righteousness" (Galatians 5:5, RSV). In the letter to the Hebrews, hope is "*the* hope" (Hebrews 3:6; 6:18, 19, emphasis supplied).

The objective of all hope is the drawing near of "the Day" (Hebrews 10:25). This day is the second coming of Jesus Christ, variously designated in the Revised Standard Version as "the day of the Lord" (Acts 2:20; 1 Thessalonians 5:2; 2 Thessalonians 2:2; 2 Peter 3:10), "the day of Jesus Christ" (Philippians 1:6), "the day of visitation"(1 Peter 2:12), "that day" (Matthew 7:22; 2 Thessalonians 1:10), or "the last day" (John 6:39, 40, 44, 54; 11:24; 12:48).

The goal of the blessed Advent hope is being eternally with the Lord following the Second Coming (1 Thessalonians 4:17). This hope for a future of uninterrupted communion and reunification with God has several major implications for the believers' present life.

Let us consider one of these major implications—the believer's response. The Bible is very explicit about the response that hope causes in the believer: "Beloved, we are God's children now; it does not yet appear what we shall be, but we know that when he appears we shall be like him, for we shall see him as he is. And everyone who thus hopes in him purifies himself as he is pure" (1 John 3:2, 3, RSV). Here the apostle makes a statement about our purification now in view of what we hope to be in the future. Thus John refutes the claim that the Christian hope can be held without reference to one's own present morality and ethics. The prospects of seeing Christ when He comes and of being at that time like He is motivate everyone who has this hope to purify themselves now through the available means that God has graciously provided.

This purification experience is an aspect of the life lived with and under God and by the power of God in the new covenant. The believer's hope is grounded in the covenant God and receives meaning from the covenant God. From the perspective of the covenant, at least two things become evident: (1) Hope is an intrinsic part of the total pattern of divine action and human response. The believer, as a member of the covenant community, responds to the God of hope in appropriate words and deeds that reflect his or her commitment to the Lord of the covenant. (2) The covenant community is made up of two parties, both characterized by hope. On the one hand, there is the "God of hope" and, on the other hand, the believer, a being of hope, who has received hope from the God of hope. It thus follows that the covenant community is a community of hope, a community of hope through God. It is a community of hope made up of individuals who receive their hope from God. It is also a community of hope in God's future. The covenant community's hope is a hope without illusion because it is grounded in the God of hope and rests upon the dependability of God.

The believers' hope that "we shall always be with the Lord" (1 Thessalonians 4:17, RSV) includes a second implication about how believers live the present life: we are living in a stance of patient waiting, enduring perseverance, and unfaltering loyalty. While waiting for the coming of the glory of God when He appears the second time, believers are calm and unworried (compare Isaiah 40:31; 41:1)—but not inactive. The divine grace provides new power for everyday life, power strong enough to withstand the severest temptations and strong enough to endure the most testing trials. Our hope in God is the source for unfaltering loyalty to God. We who have been born again to a "living hope" (1 Peter 1:3, RSV) to obtain an "imperishable, undefiled, and unfading" inheritance (verse 4, RSV) will live a life of sober obedience and godlike holiness (Hebrews 12:1–17).

Further, the hope of Christ's second coming, a hope resting in God's new covenant, brings new reality to the great commission given by the risen Christ to His disciples: "Go ye therefore, and teach all nations, baptizing them in the name of the Father, and of the Son, and of the Holy Ghost: teaching them to observe all things whatsoever I have commanded you: and, lo, I am with you alway, even unto the end of the world" (Matthew 28:19, 20). This command implies that the covenant community, built on the new covenant ratified and exemplified in Jesus Christ, becomes a community of mission. Its mission is to teach all nations the good news of Jesus Christ—what He accomplished by His perfect life, death on the cross, resurrection, and High-Priestly ministry—and the crowning good news of His soon coming, which brings all the hope of Scripture to complete fulfillment.

The central focus and personal application of this good news is that the "man of Christ" can become a new creation (2 Corinthians 5:17; compare Romans 6:4), can bear the fruits of the new life (Galatians 5:19–23; compare Ephesians 5:9), and can act in the power of the risen

Lord, performing the will of God (Ephesians 6:6). Accordingly, the life of the believer is one that he lives *for* Christ and one God can vouch for (Romans 6:11, 13; 2 Corinthians 5:15).

The promise of the Risen One, "I am with you alway" (Matthew 28:20), is the marvelous covenant promise of the constant presence of Christ. The living presence of Jesus Christ in our hearts is the climactic word of assurance that transforms present reality, making the coming face-to-face meeting with the Lord at His second coming a faith certainty that transcends all other certainties.

---

1. *New Encyclopaedia Britannica Macropaedia*, vol. 10, 1980, s.v. "life."

2. Richard M. Lemmon, *Encyclopedia Americana*, vol. 17 (Danbury, CT: Grolier, 1998), s.v. "life."

3. G. L. Borchert, "Gnosticism," *Evangelical Dictionary of Theology*, ed., Walter A. Elwell (Grand Rapids, MI: Baker Book House, 1984), 444–447; Hans Jonas, *The Gnostic Religion: The Message of the Alien God and the Beginnings of Christianity*, 2nd ed. (Boston: Beacon Press, 1963); Robert M. Grant, *Gnosticism and Early Christianity*, rev. ed. (New York: Harper and Row, 1959).